Maine's Most Scenic Roads

25 ROUTES OFF THE BEATEN PATH

2nd Edition

John Gibson
Photographs by Dianna Rust

ISBN 978-089272942-5

Designed by Phil Schirmer
Cover photo by Laurence Parent
Back cover photo by Jason Verschoor/iStockphoto

2 4 6 8 9 7 5 3 1

Library of Congress Cataloging-in-Publication Data
Gibson, John, 1940-
Maine's most scenic roads : 25 routes off the beaten path : a
traveler's guide / John Gibson.
p. cm.
Includes index.
ISBN 978-089272942-5 (pbk.)
1. Maine—Tours. 2. Automobile travel—Maine—Guidebooks.
3. Scenic byways—Maine—Guidebooks. I. Title.
F17.3.G515 1998
917.4104'43—dc21
98-28623

CIP

contents

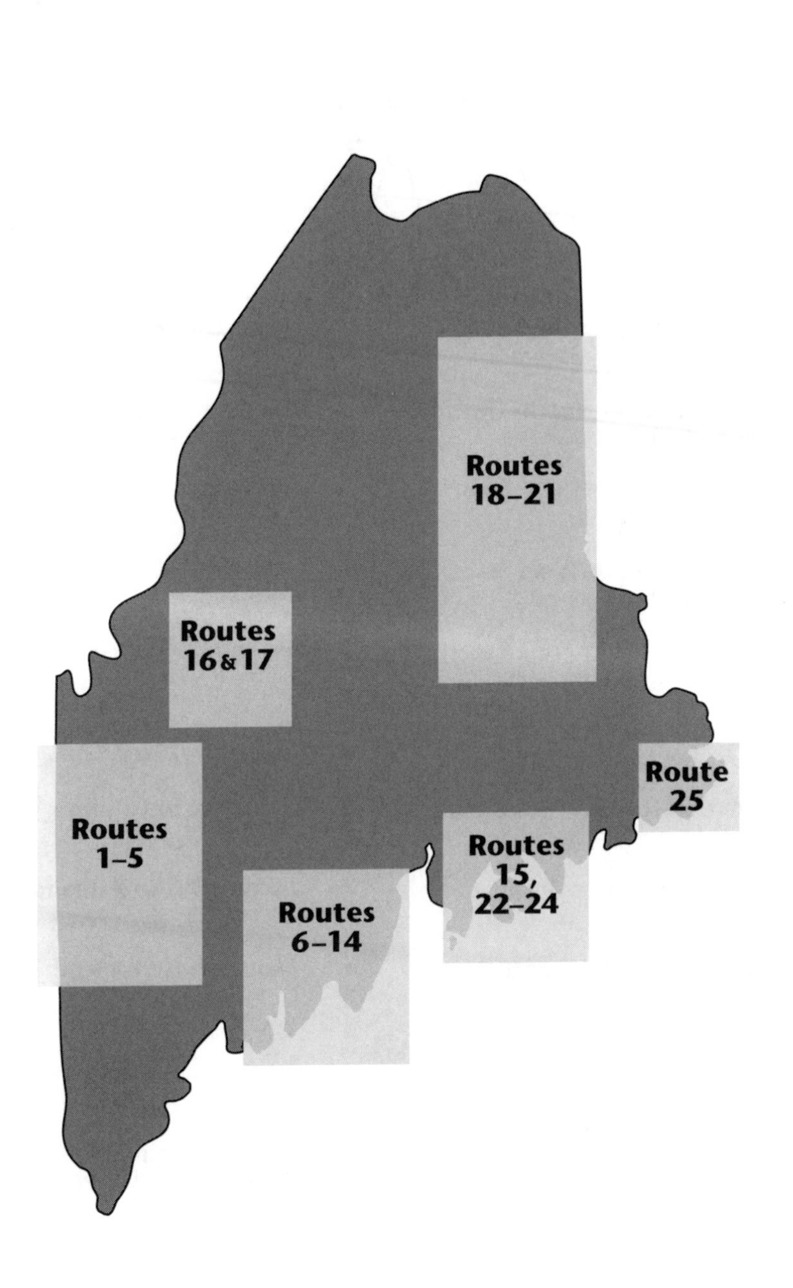
Routes
18–21
Routes
16 & 17
Route
25
Routes
1–5
Routes
15,
22–24
Routes
6–14

maps

introduction

Welcome to the inviting back roads and country highways of rural Maine. We know you'll enjoy your journey in this authentic corner of the Northeast, wherever you travel.

The Pine Tree State is a large, rangy place, and visitors are often surprised by its size when they head off to its beautiful hinterlands. This may be because Maine is the topmost part of that seemingly diminutive region known historically as New England. On a national map, New England seems a compact place, and Maine a mere section of it. Such notions can be deceptive.

If, for example, a traveler began at Kittery, the state's southernmost point, and ambled northward to the Canadian border at Fort Kent or Madawaska, he or she would drive over 300 miles before crossing that border. If you were to explore Maine from west to east, driving, for example, from Gilead to Bangor to Wesley to Machias to Lubec at the state's widest point, you would cover well over 200 miles. And every mile on every road chosen would be interesting and eye catching. Point being: There are nearly unlimited miles of open road in Maine for would-be explorers.

Maine's network of pleasant rural highways is not only extensive; it will take you through a surprising variety of landscapes. Some would say Maine has more distinct regional landscapes than any state in the nation, and they'd likely be correct. Visitors and natives alike drive the Maine coast for its legendary beauty. Small villages with salty air and the hallmarks of deepwater commerce line the way. Turn westward and you'll encounter scenic rural roads in Maine's imposing mountain country. Some of the highest and most rugged peaks in the northern Appalachians reside there. Think Saddleback, Abraham, Bigelow, Kathadin, and others.

Southern Maine drives take one to beaches, islands, and numerous necks of land that lead to striking coves and harbors. A lot of America's early history was enacted on this ground. Today, unique galleries, famous sands, crafters' studios, and artist encampments abound. Maine's great oceanfront city of Portland is here, too, rich with museums, galleries, theaters, and world-class inns and restaurants. Everything from trawlers to the world's largest ocean liners tie up on the Portland waterfront.

Go north in Maine as far as the eye can see and you'll drive through beautiful Aroostook, a place of big skies, farms, and fields, known simply to natives as "The County." Potato barns dot the countryside, seasonal storage for the county's biggest traditional crop. Silos peek over hills, and quiet roads with little traffic invite you to keep exploring. Temperatures in northern Aroostook have been seen to get rather chilly in winter, so cold, in fact, that the US Weather Service office in Caribou, Maine, routinely reports the wintriest temperatures on the national map. Drives in Aroostook show one a hard, rolling beauty found nowhere else in New England.

Motor to Newry, Rangeley, and Stratton in Maine's far northwest for bold mountain views and the best big-mountain skiing in the Northeast, plus the hospitality to go with it. Motor to Jackman and jump off from there to the sporting camps and superb fishing that make the region famous. Maine's northern lakes are thick on the vine here, and connecting rivers engage canoeists for days on end. From Rangeley to Presque Isle as the loon flies, the trout fishing in Maine's vast northwest is, as locals may allow, "wicked good." These are Maine's Great North Woods, the biggest unsettled area east of the Mississippi.

The region, visited by few from away because they haven't troubled to know about it, makes its living by harvesting lumber logs and pulp for paper. In its midst is hidden the wonder of Baxter State Park and more than 20,000 miles of gravel paper-company roads. Camping at deep woodland sites where you are quite likely to see moose, deer, fox, and bear, is available upon inquiry. Driving Maine's North Woods and tenting in the back country will put to shame any camping you've ever done in the suburban elsewhere. Maine's sporting camps are there, too, where you'll find rustic accommodations, good eating, and the best hiking, canoeing, hunting, and fishing in eastern America. As promised, you are unlikely to run out of road in Maine whatever your preferred destinations and interests.

To those who know Maine's unique terrain, it puzzles that many visitors spend so much of their travel time pursuing entertainments they might have got just as well around the corner at home. Try something different. This book urges you to get off the beaten track, leave behind the familiar, forget video games and plastic amusements, and take to Maine's open country roads. Excellent local accommodations, imaginative fine dining, grand places to "rough it" and more await you. The people you'll meet, the backbone of Maine, are finestkind, too! Yes, Interstates and major well-trafficked arteries such as U.S. Route 1 do exist in Maine. We do, in fact, have one of each. That's quite enough. This book will guide you to the many pleasing alternatives.

Practical Realities

This volume is a guide to some of Maine's most scenic rural highways, along which you'll discover much to interest you. We'll describe a host of routes you may wish to follow, some point-to-point, others loops that will bring you back to your starting point. Each route directs you to a distinct region and its flavors. Along the way we'll indicate places you may want to pause and visit, as well as shopping districts, auto services, and other important venues. Always, the purpose of each route description is to present what you will encounter as you drive along.

This isn't a guide to particular businesses or restaurants or accommodations, which may change, relocate, or close from time to time or season to season. We'll call your attention to attractions such as museums, artist and craft studios, and galleries. Places of historical and architectural interest, and scenes of natural beauty are, of course, mentioned. And, just because this is a guide to pleasant Maine drives doesn't mean we slight more energetic pastimes. Maine roads roll by many hiking trails, coastal walks, camping places, canoe launches, and excellent short strolls. We'll mention these in passing, too.

The roads talked about here generally carry only a fraction of the traffic one might find on Interstate 95 or U.S. Route 1. Occasionally, say, on a major holiday weekend, you may find more traffic than usual on these byways, but that is the rare exception, not the rule. In self-defense, Mainers peel away from the main arteries and travel these prettier rural roads whenever a holiday invasion arrives. Follow their example. In summer, you will more likely be held up by a slow-moving, tractor-drawn haywagon with kids on top than the faraway, urban variety of traffic tie-up.

In summer, weekday travel will usually accord you more of each country road to yourself than will weekends, when so many exhausted East Coast natives flock enthusiastically to Maine. You might encounter heavy traffic on U.S. Route 1 between Kittery and Ellsworth in July and August, and on the York-to-Portland stretch of I-95 on summer weekends and holidays. A little map study will suggest alternative back roads that will link you with the more welcoming country roads described herein.

Along Maine back roads buy a soda and gas up when you have a chance; don't wait till your car is running only on fumes. Strangely, people from away find it hard to believe, but lots of remote Maine villages have neither a filling station nor a supermarket, nor other such worldly amenities. Even towns with active shopping districts may not boast an open filling station or store late at night. When the day is over, Mainers like to go home and put up their feet.

At the height of the summer tourist season and around ski resorts in winter, book your overnight accommodation early, and you won't be disappointed. Same with meals. When you find an inviting backcountry restaurant that appeals, stop and have a bite. Don't automatically assume there will be another in the back of beyond just because you're surrounded by burger joints on every block back home. Away from the major population centers, Maine remains a determinedly quiet place. In some quarters of Maine, the old saw about rolling up the sidewalks at dusk may have a grain of truth in it. And then, there are those little hamlets without sidewalks.

As you enjoy making the rounds of Maine's back roads, equip yourself with a good map of the state for easy reference. (The Rand McNally Road Atlas or DeLorme Maine Atlas and Gazetteer are good choices.) The maps in this book will, of course, guide you along the routes presented, but larger maps will put regional road travel in perspective. Maps of Maine's major settled areas are also sold and will help you get around those larger towns you wish to explore. Try calling the Maine Department of Inland Fisheries and Wildlife (207-287-8000) for information about outdoor sports such as hunting and fishing. A call to the Maine Bureau of Parks and Lands (207-287-3821) will provide useful information on Maine's extensive system of state parks and camping areas.

To those who consider themselves environmentalists, urging people to drive Maine's back roads (or any roads) gives a certain pause. We live in an age of costly petroleum and concern about pollution and energy scarcity. You'll find touring more energy conscious if you keep your car well tuned, cut other nonessential driving to a minimum, maintain moderate speeds, monitor tire pressure, and drive a vehicle smaller than the Queen Mary. It's a trade-off. To enjoy driving in grand places, we need to reduce all the other unnecessary driving we do. I try to do this. I hope you will, too.

Finally, exploring Maine roads requires serious attitude adjustment. Many visitors to Maine, and some locals, roar around as if they were paid by the mile. A few even wind up embedded in trees. To enjoy roads built for comfort, not speed, you've got to proceed a little more slowly, taking time to look and enjoy, stopping here and there for whatever catches your fancy. The trip descriptions in this volume beg that one pare one's speed enough to take in the many points worth seeing along the way. One of the most appealing things about Maine is that you can set off in almost any direction down a country road and sooner or later come upon one or several scenes that will please. Whether it's your day off or an extended vacation, make the time to travel Maine roads in a leisurely fashion, seeing all there is to see. Safely.

Route 1

Fryeburg to Gilead

Highway:

Route 113 (Evans Notch Road)

Distance:

30½ miles (one way)

In a state where beautiful countryside and sturdy mountains are commonplace, one searches for appropriate words to describe travel in a region where both exceed even Maine standards. Evans Notch is a cleft in that component of the Appalachian chain that tumbles over into Maine along the state's western border. Rising above a fine intervale to its south and the Androscoggin River to its north, the Evans Notch region remains a largely undeveloped gem of mountain pasture and grand hills closely bound up with the early settlement of Maine's western mountain country.

Route 113, or the Evans Notch Road as it is often called, runs the length of this storied territory, from the pleasant academy town of Fryeburg northward to the tiny hamlet of Gilead at its junction with U.S. Route 2. Along the way a numerous opportunities to photograph, to hike, to ca

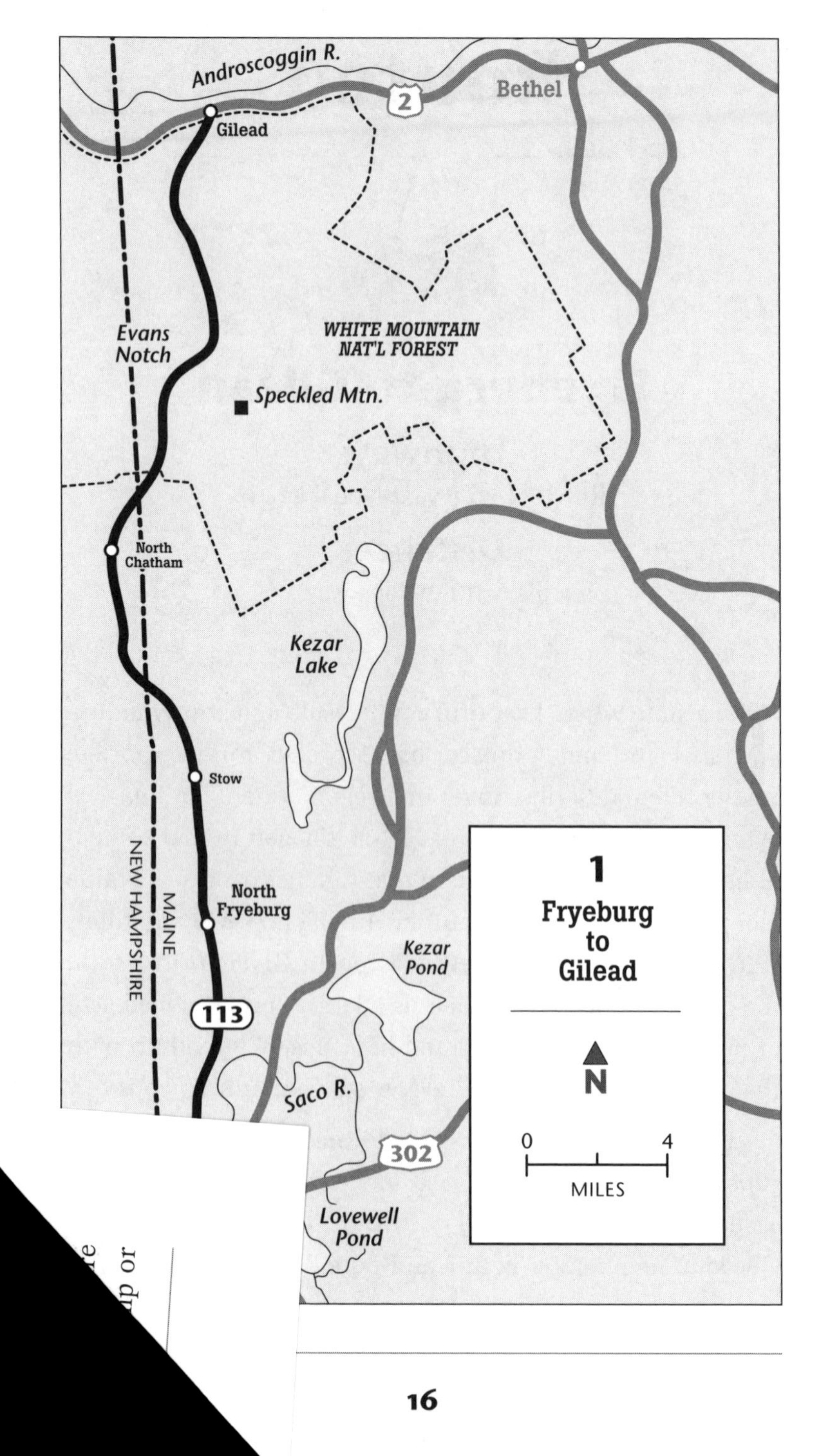

Androscoggin R.
2
Bethel
Gilead
Evans
Notch
WHITE MOUNTAIN
NAT'L FOREST
Speckled Mtn.
North
Chatham
Kezar
Lake
Stow
NEW HAMPSHIRE
MAINE
North
Fryeburg
113
Kezar
Pond
Saco R.
302
Lovewell
Pond
1
Fryeburg
to
Gilead
N
0
4
MILES

fish, to swim, or simply to lean back and take in the splendid scenery.

This journey begins where Route 113 leaves Main Street (U.S. Route 302) in Fryeburg, by the U.S. Post Office, and runs north into farm country. Leaving the residential section of town, the road soon is in farmland at the edge of a vast intervale ringed by mountains in New Hampshire and Maine. Working farms sell produce here in season. The road quickly crosses the Saco River, where there is a parking area and sand beach (swimming, canoeing) on the right, half a mile from the post office. Passing more cultivated fields, you soon reach a junction, and you bear right and north on Route 113 in a mile.

The route runs northward through settlements and more working farms on the flat intervale. At a store, the road makes a sharp turn right, and having run for a little in New Hampshire, crosses back into Maine again. The countryside becomes more sparsely settled and more wooded. A little stream appears on the right at five miles. Clumps of polypody fern and tiger lilies grow along the roadside. Farm fields appear and disappear here, and it is surprising to many travelers to see so much concentrated farming in one of New England's most prominent mountain regions.

At 6¾ miles, you'll see sheep in pasture and more cultivated fields on a curve, with the White Mountains of New Hampshire and the lower mountains of western Maine as backdrop. More fields soon offer open west-to-east vistas of mountains, horizon to horizon. At the Universalist Chapel, built in 1838, you pass Fish Street in North Fryeburg and continue northward, passing through the last built-up area (filling station) before entering the mountains. Route 113 goes left here, passes the Saco Valley Fire Station, and then rolls northward again. A few houses and small farms begin to yield to woodland, and you cross the Stow town line at just under ten miles.

Descending, the road runs through borders of stone walls, passes old farms going back to woods, and comes to the bridge over Little Cold River. Here you bear left at 11½ miles and then immediately right again by the Stow Corner Store, staying on Route 113. The road soon runs into New Hampshire as striking views ahead to the notch appear beyond the Stow Baptist Church. More views build to the northeast as you progress, passing the Stow (1842) Town Hall. Stands of birches grow along the route, and occasional turnouts offer expanding views to the north and east at 12¾ miles.

The road becomes more hilly as you get closer to the mountains. Spruce and balsam appear in denser woods. You pass a few isolated farms surrounded by mountains on all sides. Cresting a rise, you continue north on Route 113 as Route 113B comes in on the left from Chatham Center, New Hampshire, at nearly fifteen miles. Shortly, large old farmhouses appear in the northernmost reaches of the intervale. At 16¾ miles, at a "Windagon" sign on the right, you pass the gravel road that runs through to Evergreen Valley and Lovell.

You'll see the attractive profile of Deer Hill to the right across a field after passing Chandler Farm. Striking views toward the imposing Baldface summits appear on the left, opposite the entrance to the Appalachian Mountain Club's

Cold River Camp at 17⅓ miles. The camp has been a center for hiking in the notch for more than seventy years. A hiker's parking lot lies here on the right, also.

The road now enters the last intervale before it climbs up the notch. Spectacular views from west to east reveal an uninterrupted panorama of mountains and more mountains. The last great farmhouses of the valley are left in the distance, and the ledges that front Blueberry Mountain lie off to the east. The Mount Meader Trail road is passed at a bit over 18 miles, and the long ridge along which the 28-mile Skyline Trail runs is silhouetted to the left. Fine views up through the notch toward East and West Royce Mountains appear next. The route enters woods again, and at over 19 miles a warning sign stands at the roadside, reminding us that this is not a plowed road in winter. Plows come this far and no farther. At its highest reaches, Evans Notch is cut off and buried in deep snow at the cold end of the calendar. Usually by Thanksgiving and sometimes considerably earlier, passage beyond this point for cars isn't possible till the following spring.

Along a screen of pretty white birches, you drive into the White Mountain National Forest at 19½ miles. The Basin Campground is on the left, where the road turns sharply right, crosses a stream, and arrives at the 190-year-old Brickett Place. This fine old home was built of timber by early settlers around 1816 and reconstructed of brick about 1830. The house has been open summers for inspection, with a caretaker present in recent years. The yard is the hub of a series of hiking trails that traverse the mountains above. Pull in here to the grassy parking area in front of the house.

John and Catherine Brickett came to this wild, unsettled area around 1816 to claim a piece of land within the Batchelders Grant (1807). The impressive and unusual brick house they eventually built here has been on the National Register of Historic Places since 1982. The house was for many years the last outpost in the notch and became publicly owned in 1918. It was used as a U.S. Forest Service ranger station in the 1930s and 1940s. When the Civilian Conservation Corps constructed a more modern road through the notch beginning in 1933, the corps used the Brickett Place as its headquarters during the operation.

Leaving the Brickett Place, you next bear right and continue north on Route 113, which begins to climb steeply. There are excellent views of East and West Royce Mountains through the trees to the left. The road continues to ascend, and a deep ravine appears to the left. Ledges hang next to the road at 20½ miles on the right. In the late autumn and early spring (before the snows or once the snows have melted), the views here are superb when the trees are bare. At twenty-two miles, turnouts exist on both sides of the road, where there are fine views southward down the notch. You are nearly at the height-of-land here, and pass the Laughing Lion Trail sign on the left.

Additional viewpoints are scattered along the roadside as the drive levels off and then begins to descend northward in more beautiful white birches. The angle of descent increases as you pass Spruce Hill on the right and the trailheads to East Royce Mountain and to Spruce Hill in moments. Evans Brook begins to appear on the left of the roadside, sometimes screened by brush.

You can take your foot off the gas pedal here, and your vehicle will roll for miles, so great is the downhill grade. At 24⅓ miles you'll cross a stream and enter the Haystack–Speckled Mountain Wilderness. At 25¾ miles you come to the hidden parking area for Caribou Mountain trails (restroom facilities in summer) on the right.

Continuing, lovely Evans Brook is fully visible on the left as it parallels the road. At 26¾ miles you go by the road into Peabody Mountain on the right. Route 113 immediately crosses Evans Brook as you enter the area known as Hastings, named after two brothers engaged in logging in the region around the turn of the century. The attractive and secluded Hastings Campground is in a grove of trees to the right at 27¼ miles. A gravel road that runs southwest to another camping area along Wild River is on the left, and then you arrive at the dramatic junction of Evans Brook and Wild River, both fed by runoff and snowmelt from the surrounding mountains. Wild River, the bigger of the two boulder-strewn watercourses, has its origins in the Carter-Mahoosuc Range to the west in New Hampshire. At the junction of the rivers, to the right of the road, is the Roost Trail, an easily walkable footpath that climbs quickly to the Roost, a precipice with good views of the northern end of the notch.

Meandering through several bends, the road descends some more, following the river. After passing a number of turnouts with striking water views, at 28½ miles you exit the White Mountain National Forest. Crossing still another feeder stream, you will see some exaggerated bends in the Wild River as it trends northwest. The river divides and then shortly enters a single channel again. Soon, you'll come upon several cabins near the road, the first human settlement since the other end of the notch. At 30½ miles, you reach the end of this route as Route 113 joins U.S. Route 2 in the little town of Gilead. A public picnic area is located just east on U.S. Route 2. Cabin accommodations are available in season at the road junction.

Route 2

Bethel, Grafton Notch, and Upton

Highway:

Route 26

Distance:

24½ miles (one way on Grafton Notch Road)

Louise Dickinson Rich extolled the virtues of this corner of Maine in books such as *We Took to the Woods* and *My Neck of the Woods*. The nearly wild flavor of northwestern Maine has changed since she wrote her tributes to the region in the 1940s, but not all that much. In fact, once one pulls away from the settled precincts of Bethel and nearby ski areas, the journey northward through Grafton Notch to the tiny crossroads of Upton takes one back into a landscape little altered.

Northwestern Maine remains sparsely settled, and the route described here follows a winding path through truly rugged country, a majestic range of uplands including some of Maine's higher mountains. This heavily wooded area is full of still untrammeled places like Andover North Surplus,

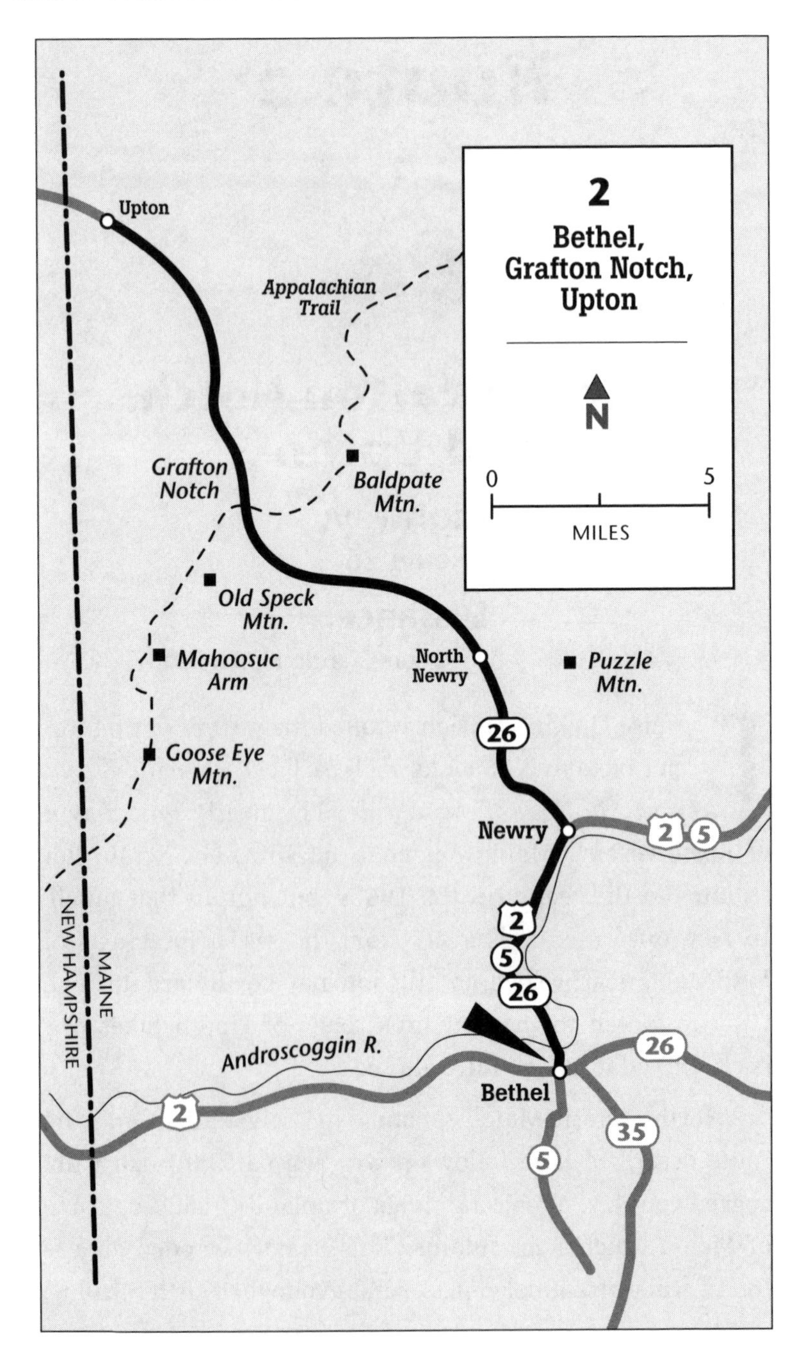
2
Bethel,
Grafton Notch,
Upton
N
0
5
MILES
Upton
Appalachian
Trail
Grafton
Notch
Baldpate
Mtn.
Old Speck
Mtn.
Mahoosuc
Arm
Goose Eye
Mtn.
North
Newry
Puzzle
Mtn.
26
Newry
2
5
2
5
26
Androscoggin R.
Bethel
26
2
35
5
NEW HAMPSHIRE
MAINE

Township C, and C Surplus. Interlocked mountains and lakes combine to make this one of the most scenic territories in New England.

The route driven here begins in the small, attractive college community of Bethel, about fifteen miles east of the New Hampshire border. Bethel is home to Gould Academy, one of Maine's fine preparatory schools, and the campus, a worthy place for a stroll, lies within the center of the town. On the north side of the settled area look for Route 26 (the Mayville Road), which runs north and east toward Rumford. Take this highway out of town and cross the pretty Androscoggin River. Inns and bed-and-breakfast establishments line the highway here.

Excellent views of mountain ranges to the northeast and east lie ahead, and pleasing outlooks over the meandering Androscoggin River appear from time to time. Driving along an intervale, you continue northward, passing the entry road to Sunday River Ski Resort on the left in North Bethel. A picnic area overlooking the Androscoggin lies to the right shortly. Continuing northeastward, the road crosses the Sunday River and, later, the Bear River, in the direction of Newry. Fine open country appears, dotted with pines, and backed with mountains and farms. Five and one-half miles beyond the entrance road to the ski area, turn left at Grafton Notch State Park signs, where Route 26 (Bear River Road) leaves Route 5, and head north. Set your odometer here.

The land unfolds now amidst fields, with splendid views ahead toward Sunday River Whitecap and Old Speck. Passing the Bear River Grange, the road rises quickly as you enter real mountain country to the northwest. Ledgy outcrops appear on mountainsides. Five miles up Bear River Road, you pass the Newry Town Offices on the left in a pretty intervale. The road runs sharply to the northeast with more mountain views ahead as you continue to rise. Another intervale offers excellent views toward the mountains to the northwest, fronted by old farms. Crossing a pretty stream with a footbridge, you come to the Newry Community Church after traveling eight miles on the road to the Notch.

You continue to climb here as the route brings you closer to Grafton Notch. Cliffs and slides are visible northeastward on Mount Hittie and Lightning Ledge. Behind these rises are the two higher peaks of rangy Baldpate Mountain. To the northwest, Sunday River Whitecap and massive Old Speck are now clearly in view. Mahoosuc Guide Service is on the right, 10¼ miles up the Notch Road. Beautiful open fields lie here in the intervale. Wight Brook Reserve also lies to the right at 10¾ miles.

A pretty little stream on the left under fine westward views marks the entrance to Grafton Notch State Park at 11½ miles. Brooding, 4,200-foot Old Speck looms closer ahead. Climbing higher into the notch you rise more steeply at 12¼ miles. Shortly you'll find Screw Augur Falls to the left. Pause and visit this site to witness a series of incredible basins and channels gouged into Maine granite by millennia of water action. Less than a mile farther on to the right you will see parking for Mother Walker Falls Gorge, another geologically interesting feature worth inspection. Moose Cave Gorge is a few hundred yards farther north.

You crest the height-of-land in just over fourteen miles, and soon, to the right, are the ledges of Table Rock, a large outcrop on Baldpate Mountain to which there is a trail. Dramatic views of glistening ledges on Old Speck appear now, and, after 15 miles on this road, you reach the Old Speck parking area where the 2,000-mile-long Appalachian Trail crosses Route 26. This is an active hiking center for climbs up Old Speck and Baldpate, and to Table Rock. Behind Old Speck lies a network of trails into the Mahoosuc Range, with some of the most rugged hiking in the entire Appalachian chain. Mountain views from this parking area are impressive.

The route continues northward beyond the Appalachian Trail crossing. Densely forested lands of spruce and fir dominate as you reach the Spruce Meadow Picnic Area on the left at sixteen miles, where there are open views of the weather-wracked north slopes of Old Speck. At seventeen miles you exit the boundaries of the state park and descend through moose country to the northwest. Conifers begin to give way to deciduous trees as spruce and hackmatack mix with oak, maple, ash, and birch. The road levels off somewhat at nineteen miles. Norway and blue spruce, hackmatack, and white pine line the highway again in what is unsettled, wild timber country. Bogs lie in depressions to the east as the road follows a ridgeline.

At just under twenty-one miles, you cross the Upton town line, climbing a bit again. Even though you have been descending steadily, you're still high up here, as will be abundantly clear in a moment. You soon reach the tiny village of Upton, an outpost once home to nearly two hundred, now not much more than a crossroads. Maine writer Louise Dickinson Rich lived here for several winters with her children when not at her woodland home on the Rapid River. She wrote interestingly of Upton and the lands around Umbagog in *Happy the Land* (1944).

One has a sense of being north of north here when passing the town offices and the Upton Grange at twenty-four miles. A few hundred yards beyond you come to a place with spectacular views to the north, high over Umbagog Lake and the Richardson Lakes, and toward the Rangeley Lakes. Pull over on the gravel shoulder and enjoy this scene—one of the best in New England.

This has long been timber country, and the expansive lakes and adjacent rivers below were the scene of many log drives. These northern waters were also home to some of the finest trout and salmon fishing in the Northeast for many years. "Sports" and their families came to this country over a network of narrow-gauge railroads at the turn of the century. The railroads, the great summer hotels and colonies, are now largely gone, replaced by smaller private camps and lodges.

This route description concludes here, but travelers can continue into New Hampshire on Route 26, just beyond Upton, or reverse direction and enjoy the return trip down through Grafton Notch, where new views emerge as one travels southward.

Route 3

Norway-Harrison-Bridgton-Lovell-Waterford-Harrison

Highway:

Routes 117, 93, 5, 35

Distance:

54½ miles (around loop)

This journey drifts westward from Norway, an attractive town in a region of lakes, ponds, and rolling hills. The route makes a loop around some major lakes, over hills and ridges, through western mountains, and back again via attractive villages on backcountry ponds. The circuit lends itself to summer and autumn driving, when the lakes and hills are in their most appealing colors. In September and October this journey carries one through miles of brilliant autumn foliage on country lanes that are sparsely settled and little trafficked.

A major shopping and service center in Maine's southwestern corner, Norway is one of a diminishing number of communities that still possess a genuine main street with traditional storefronts. I like the feel of such places. Drivi

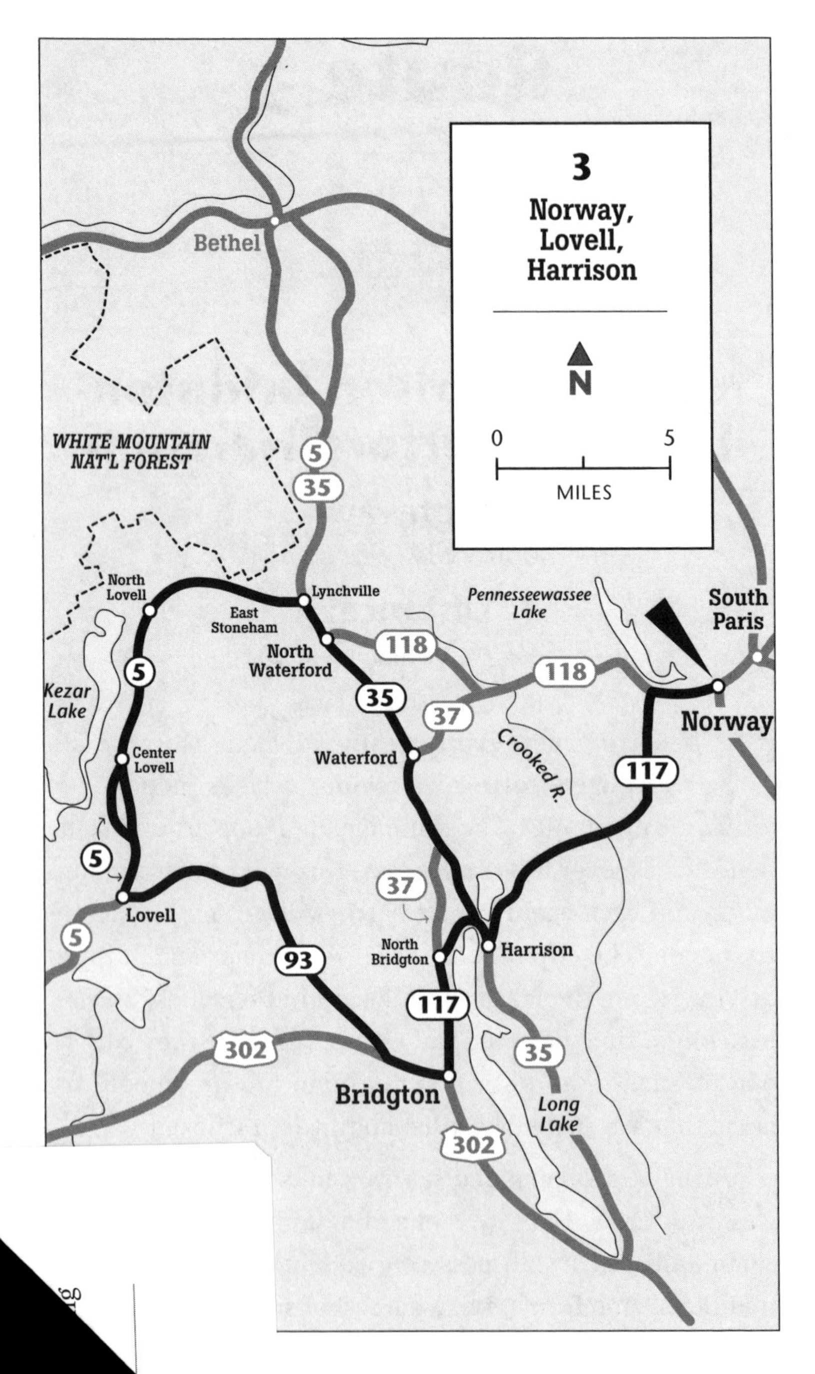
3
Norway, Lovell, Harrison
N
0
5
MILES
Bethel
WHITE MOUNTAIN NAT'L FOREST
5
35
North Lovell
East Stoneham
Lynchville
North Waterford
Pennesseewassee Lake
South Paris
118
118
35
37
Norway
Kezar Lake
Center Lovell
Waterford
Crooked R.
117
5
37
Lovell
5
93
North Bridgton
Harrison
117
302
35
Bridgton
Long Lake
302

northward up Main Street, you pass the Norway Memorial Library, the offices of the *Advertiser Democrat* and Oxford Hills Press, and the First Universalist Church. Leaving the north end of town on Route 117, set your odometer to zero as soon as Pennesseewassee Lake comes into view ahead on the right. This attractive body of water stretches northwest, backed by fine mountain views. In minutes, on the left, you'll find a sheltered state picnic area overlooking the water.

Go left and south next, staying with Route 117 and drawing away from the lake in the direction of Bridgton in wooded countryside. Low ground here is host to swamp maples, brilliant when in autumn color. At 4 miles, you briefly pass through a more settled area, and, running through open country once again, come to the Otisfield town line at a bit over 5 miles. Running more west and northwest, you drop to the Twin Bridges state rest area at 6¼ miles. Here the road crosses the attractive Crooked River, which flows from origins way up in Songo Pond, south of Bethel. Sections of the Crooked offer good trout fishing. Here you cross the Harrison town line, too.

After a westward climb, you crest a hill at seven miles and pull to the southwest as mountains appear ahead, with views of the ski-trailed slopes of Pleasant Mountain in distant Bridgton. Soon you pass Frosty Hollow Farm at just over 9 miles, go by some open fields, and descend along the pretty shoreline of Crystal Lake. In minutes you round a bend and are in the center of Harrison at 11½ miles. Harrison is a pleasant, small resort community at the north end of beautiful Long Lake. It offers accommodations, swimming and boating, restaurants, and fuel services.

Taking in good views down Long Lake to your left, stay on Route 117 as it crosses a stream and roll south toward Bridgton. At 12½ miles you cross the Bridgton town line. At the junction of Routes 117 and 37 you pass a swim beach on the left and, on the right, the campus of Bridgton Academy. Commercial camping facilities are located along the west side of Long Lake at 14⅓ miles. Some mountain views appear again at just under sixteen miles, where you drop downhill to the junction of Route 117 and US Route 302 in Bridgton.

Bear right on U.S. Route 302 and drive west on Bridgton's main street. This once sleepy town has come back to life, particularly in summer, when it is host to many visitors in nearby resorts and camps. Interesting shops, restaurants, and a nostalgic movie house are available. Follow U.S. Route 302 uphill and to the right at just over seventeen miles by the Bridgton House and monument. You'll pass various tourist accommodations with water views along here, and soon take a right on Route 93. This quiet country road follows the west shore of Highland Lake northwest toward Sweden and Lovell. On Route 93 you crest Green Hill before long, in mixed-growth forest and great clusters of roadside ferns, next crossing the Sweden town line at 22 miles.

Stone walls border both sides of the road, and you turn sharply to the right at a junction with Plummer Hill Road, staying on Route 93. You climb another ridge with big stands of red oak, and pass open fields with white paper birches, where there are good outlooks east and west to surrounding hills. Passing the Sweden Community Meeting House and the Sweden Community Church, Route 93 comes to a crossroads soon, where you go left on Lovell Road by two lovely colonial houses. There are some good rightward views here down through pasture to scenic Keys Pond.

More hilly, sparsely settled country dominates the way as you next drive westward toward Lovell. At just under 27 miles, spectacular views west and north to the mountains of western Maine and New Hampshire open up briefly as the road runs over Popple Hill. The way descends steadily southwest and west, and you enter Lovell at 29 miles. The fragrant smell of a nearby sawmill hangs in the air as you arrive at the little junction where Route 93 joins Route 5. Go right and north here by the Millbank Manor and pass the post office, some shops, and a school. Route 5 runs up a hill past this little cluster of houses and is soon in open country.

Route 5 heads north through Center Lovell, Bryant Hill, and North Lovell, staying east and above the long north-south expanse of Kezar Lake. The lake, home to a number of cottage colonies, is visible occasionally. Fine mountain views open up to the west in a moment as you go past the Center Lovell Inn. At 34 miles a road leads right from Center Lovell to Sabattus Mountain, where an easy, short walk will take you to the summit. At 37 miles the climb northward continues over Bryant Hill as you reach the north end of Kezar Lake. You descend into North Lovell and the entrance road to Evergreen Valley at 38¼ miles. A wide network of hiking trails to the high mountains just west of here leaves the Evergreen Valley area, with access from this side road. Passing the Lewis Dana Hill Library on the right, Route 5 shortly enters Stoneham at 39½ miles.

On the left, in moments, you pass strikingly lovely Keewaydin Lake, following the winding lakeshore.

Keewaydin is surrounded on all sides by mountains. Drifting next through tiny East Stoneham, where you pass the post office at 42½ miles, you cross the Albany Township line (fine mountain views in your rearview mirror) and come next to Lynchville, where Routes 5 and 35 turn north. You continue eastward on Route 35. In another mile you arrive at a junction with Route 118 in North Waterford, where you keep right and southeast on Route 35 at 44½ miles. Climb past the North Waterford Post Office. More good mountain outlooks are behind you here as you drive along between old stone walls.

The Waterford Fire Department and Town Offices are on the right at 47½ miles, and you begin to descend slightly toward the southeast in very pretty countryside. At 49 miles is the Kedarburn Inn. Descending still, you then come to a junction, keeping right by the Lake House, and driving through the attractive village of Waterford with its fine old houses. On the left is Keoka Lake, along which the road now travels. The route turns more to the south past the lake and soon comes to the old Wesleyan Chapel at 50½ miles, where you stay left at a fork on Routes 35 and 37. Bear Pond lies to the right; Bear and Hawk Mountains rise to your immediate left. Keep left again, on Route 35, as Routes 35 and 37 divide at just under 52 miles. The Bear River parallels the road to the right.

Here the road makes its final descent through white pine and red oak growth toward Harrison, arriving again at its junction with Route 117 at the head of Long Lake in a few minutes. Our journey ends here, by the Harrison House, after 54½ miles.

Route 4

Wilton to Weld and Mount Blue State Park

Highway:

Routes 156 (Center Hill Road), 142 (West Road)

Distance:

13½ miles (one way), plus optional local travel

Were this one of those forgettable travelogues shown on very late-night television, this route might well be called the highway to the clouds. Better judgment will reign, however, and the traveler is simply advised that here's one of the most scenic forays into Maine's western mountains that can be had for a short drive. This is a hilly outing, both as to roads driven and sights seen.

The route begins east of Wilton's shopping district at the junction of Route 156 and Main Street. Follow Route 156 (the Weld Road) north out of town, soon passing the former manufacturing facilities of G.H. Bass Company on your left.

The road rises quickly out of town and runs by a golf course at approximately four miles. Wilson Stream appears on the left in low ground. The settled area yields quickly to

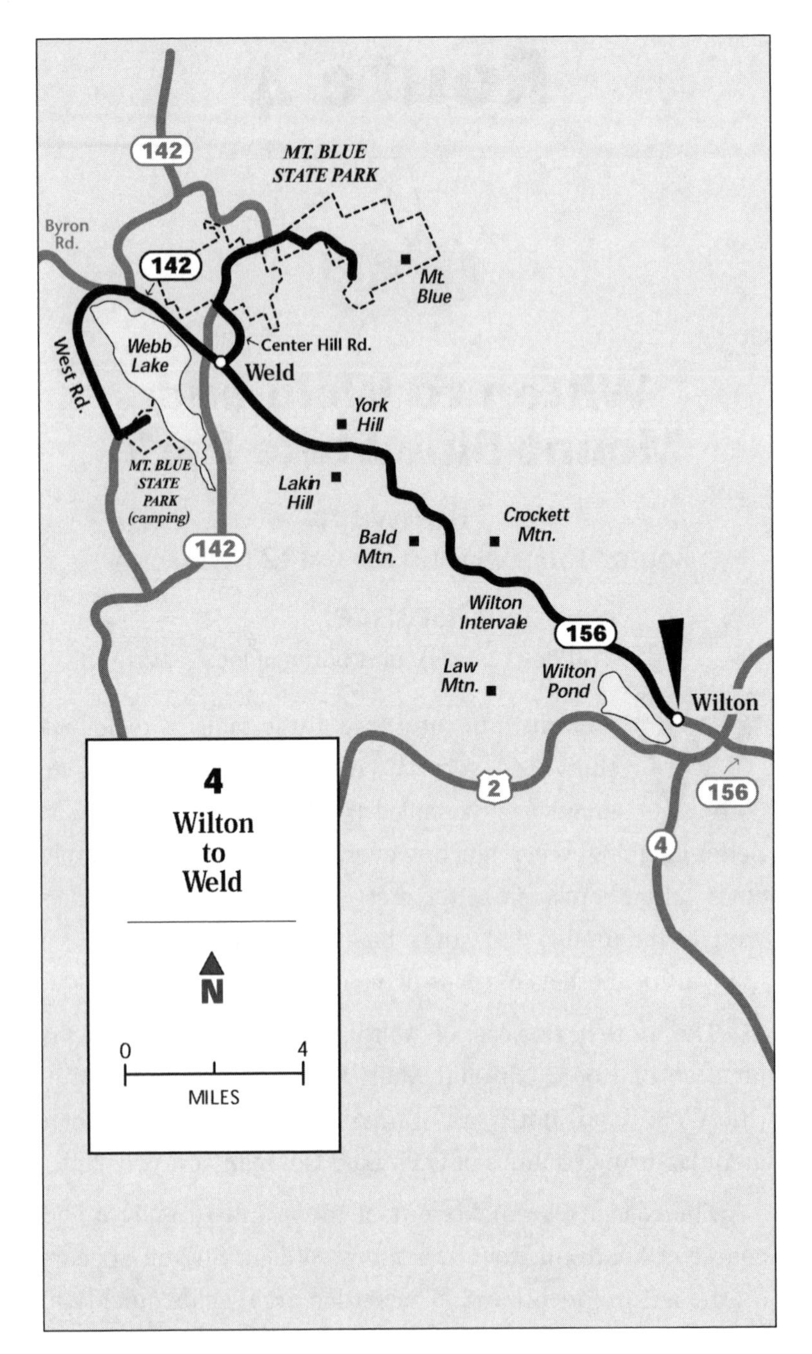
142
MT. BLUE
STATE PARK
Byron
Rd.
142
Mt.
Blue
Center Hill Rd.
Webb
Lake
Weld
West Rd.
York
Hill
MT. BLUE
STATE
PARK
(camping)
Lakin
Hill
Crockett
Mtn.
Bald
Mtn.
142
Wilton
Intervale
156
Law
Mtn.
Wilton
Pond
Wilton
2
156
4
4
Wilton
to
Weld
N
0
4
MILES

The view eastward to Mount Blue over Lake Webb

open fields and a number of small farms scattered along the road. Early mountain views to the north are visible here and there, providing a taste of what is to come.

Rolling through pretty countryside, you begin a gradual, winding climb northwestward. The road traverses the Wilton Intervale between Law Mountain and Crockett Mountain. At six miles you leave Wilton and cross into Washington Township. This little-settled road now curves freely through the hill country, ascending steadily. A mix of evergreens and deciduous trees makes this area extremely colorful in autumn. Openings in foliage offer broader, dramatic views to the mountains around Weld.

The bold, rugged shape of Bald Mountain, sometimes referred to as Saddleback Wind, can be seen in minutes on the left. Though unmarked, a clear hiking trail leads to the open summit. At roughly nine miles, watch for the trailhead by a turnout with several boulders on your left on a curve. This hike offers excellent views northward over the Lake Webb area. Just past the trailhead, find lovely Halls Pond on your left. Further views open up over the pond southwest to Bald Mountain.

Heading more to the west, Route 156 wends its way between Lakin Hill and York Hill, now in Perkins Township. The road reaches its peak in this section and shortly begins its descent into Weld. At about 10½ miles watch for a roadside spring on your right, where fresh drinking water is usually available. The approach to Weld takes us past some farms, pleasant older homes, and the village school. Ahead are the mountains that ring this small, quiet town. You arrive at Weld center by the general store at the junction of Routes 156 and 142 after driving 13½ miles.

Options:

Several local roads will take you to spectacular perches around Weld, where the beauty of the region is fully evident. First, bear right on Center Hill Road and follow it east and north just under two miles, where a turnout offers spectacular views westward over Lake Webb and Spruce Mountain, and of Tumbledown and Little Jackson Mountains on the Byron Notch Road to the northwest.

If you're a hiker, continue along Center Hill Road, which becomes dirt just around the bend and meanders eastward nearly four miles farther to the grassy trailhead parking area at Mount Blue. (The last two miles of this gravel road are rough, but definitely passable for passenger cars.) The hike up the mountain is a steep but short 1½ miles, and marvelous outlooks all over western Maine are scattered around the brushy summit.

Returning to Weld village center, go north on Route 142 (the Phillips Road) and continue to Weld Corner, bearing left onto West Road. Follow this pretty, narrow road around to the fields at the north end of Lake Webb. Passing Byron Notch Road, you soon find striking views southward down the lake. Continue west and south on West Road, where you rise to superb views across Lake Webb toward the distinctive outline of Mount Blue. These are arguably among the finest lake and mountain scenes in New England.

Continue down West Road to the end of this route, the camping section of Mount Blue State Park. In season, there are excellent camping, swimming, and boating facilities here on well-managed state lands. Additional picnicking sites are available on the gravel approach road to Mount Blue, described earlier. In high summer, campsite reservations should be made in advance with the Maine Bureau of Parks and Lands in Augusta (207-287-3821).

Appalachian Mountain Club maps, available locally, cover hikes in this region. See also Chloe Chunn's *50 Hikes in the Maine Mountains* (Backcountry Publications).

Route 5

Rumford to Rangeley

Highway:
Routes 17, 4, 16

Distance:
42 miles (one way)

Here's a journey that winds its way up the western spine of the Pine Tree State in the rough lake and mountain country that's brought a well-worn fame to this remote Maine region. Along the way are some of the most dramatic views of wild, mountainous countryside anywhere in the Northeast. From Rumford, on the Androscoggin, to the Rangeley Lakes, this route rises into the territory of Maine's big mountains, old lumber camps, legendary lake and stream fishing, boating, comfortable local accommodations, big-woods hiking, and more. Smack up against the Canadian border, this corner of north-western Maine shows little development, and its approach to tourism has remained, thankfully, very low-key.

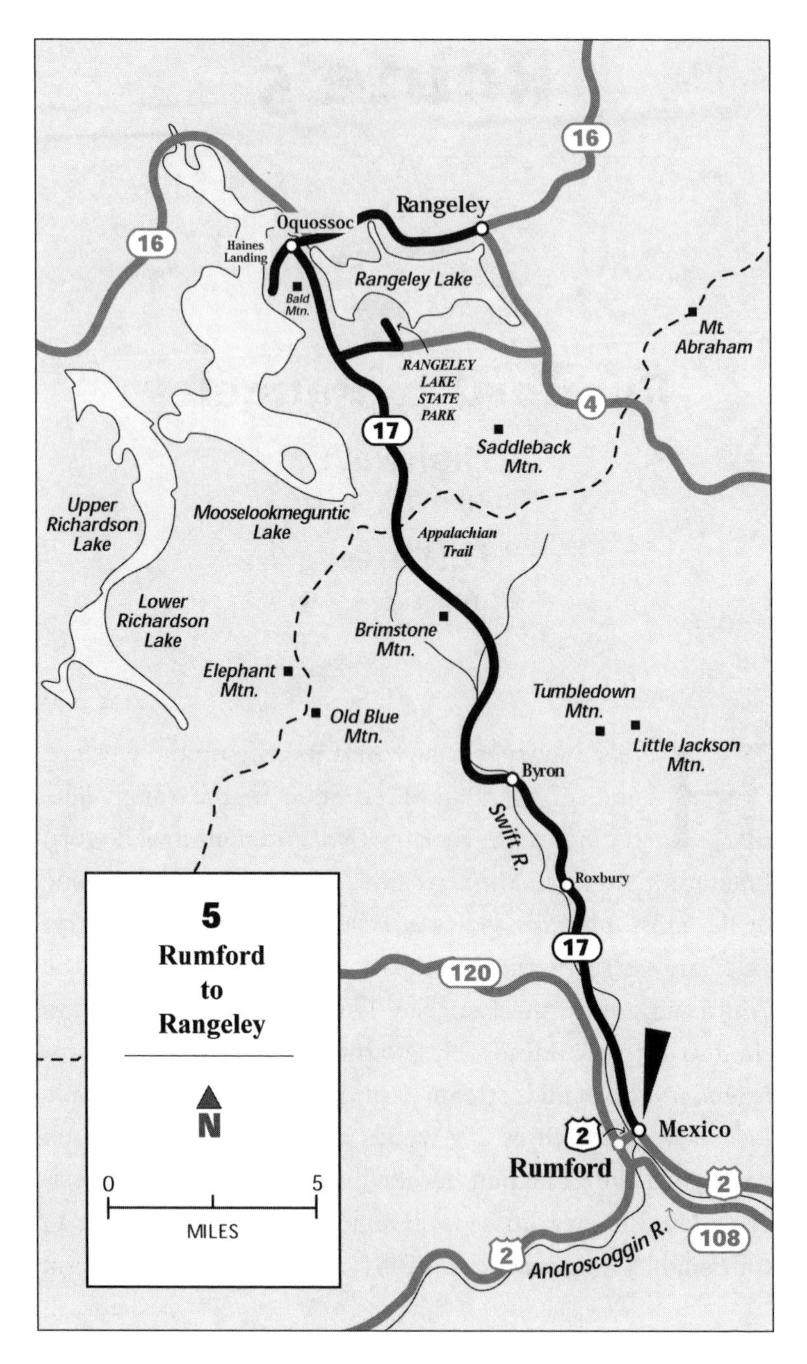
Rangeley
Oquossoc
Haines Landing
16
16
Rangeley Lake
Bald Mtn.
Mt. Abraham
RANGELEY LAKE STATE PARK
4
17
Saddleback Mtn.
Upper Richardson Lake
Mooselookmeguntic Lake
Appalachian Trail
Lower Richardson Lake
Brimstone Mtn.
Elephant Mtn.
Old Blue Mtn.
Tumbledown Mtn.
Little Jackson Mtn.
Byron
Swift R.
Roxbury
17
120
5
Rumford to Rangeley
N
0
5
MILES
Mexico
2
Rumford
2
108
2
Androscoggin R.

Though the route described here can be followed year-round, it is probably best traveled in late spring, summer, and early autumn. This is snow country, meaning that early storms in October are not uncommon on the northern end of the drive. Equally, snow lingers late in some years, and it may be April before the mountainside stretches of this road are completely bare of snow and ice.

Rumford itself is a pleasant town with its own main street of shops and services west of the mill district. Our trip begins across the river in Mexico, in the shadow of Rumford's giant paper mill complex. Set your odometer to zero and drive north from the junction of U.S. Route 2 with Route 17 in Mexico. Running through a residential district, Route 17 heads out into more rural country in two miles, with occasional views ahead to mountains. The Swift River, which this road follows all the way north to Byron and Township E, appears through brush in a ravine to the left. In 3¾ miles, stream meanders and cultivated fields are visible to the northwest. A roadside sign remarks, quite truthfully, this is "A Maine Scenic Highway."

The route follows an intervale dotted with fields being hayed in summer and passes a road over to Andover and South Arm at 5½ miles. You drive closer to the Swift River now, with views of the ledgy watercourse at just under seven miles. Soon you are in tiny Roxbury, passing the little fire station on the left. Beautiful mountain views open up to the left shortly, with more stream views at ten miles. After Roxbury, the route becomes more winding and ranges up and down, crossing a number of streams. Big mountain views well ahead up the notch appear in the direction of

Rangeley. A bold red fox bolted across the road in front of me on my last drive here past a cluster of farmhouses in still another intervale.

Crossing the Swift River shortly, at thirteen miles, you arrive in Byron at Coos Canyon on the right, a spectacular gorge carved out by the river as it charges southward. There is a small state park reservation here and opportunity to walk around and view the gorge from various points. If you arrive in late summer, the river will be low and the falls muted. In spring, choked with snowmelt runoff, Coos Canyon is a place of raging water and breakneck falls. In the low-water season, people climb down to the riverbed and cool off in rocky pools. (Use extreme caution if you attempt this.) A campground lies across the road from the gorge.

The route continues to climb northward at 14¼ miles, following the river, which becomes more visible gradually and is wider and shallower, riven by gravel bars. Shortly before the road crosses into Township E, the river divides at Houghton, the Swift going right and its West Branch going left. Soon after, another watercourse, Berdeen Stream, comes in on the left. Entering Township E at nineteen miles, you'll see Mott Stream on the right side of the winding road. Then, to the left, in Township D, rises Brimstone Mountain. You are traveling now in blessedly wild country, not a store or dwelling (or gas pump) in sight. Scenic Beaver Pond is on the left, in minutes.

At twenty miles you sense the subtle but steady climb ahead of you. The road curves and climbs more quickly in the next several miles, passing Ten Degree, a mere point on the mountainous map. The great hulk of 3,700-foot Elephant

Mountain lies off to the west, an isolated stopping place on the Appalachian Trail. The road widens after crossing the trail, and you arrive at Summit after 24½ miles, a turnout on Route 17 with superb views over Maine's most fabled lakes region.

Upper and Lower Richardson Lakes and Mooselookmeguntic Lake are the great bodies of water in sight. My father patrolled these densely wooded shores as a Maine Forest Service warden in the 1930s. Cupsuptic Lake and Aziscohos Lake lie in the distant northwest and north, the former fed by the Toothaker brooks and Kennebago River. One can stop at this roadside place on a quiet afternoon and observe for a long time, new surprises opening up to the eye for as long as one is patient. I know of no finer roadside lake and mountain views anywhere in the Northeast.

The road climbs some more, with occasional views as it reenters woods, heading northward toward Oquossoc. You enter Rangeley Plantation at just under twenty-six miles, with the road sticking to the high ground. A long up-and-down run begins, and views open up to the great mountains to the east at twenty-nine miles. Watch for a right-hand turnout soon, with excellent views eastward over Rangeley Lake toward Rangeley village and Saddleback Mountain. In the far distance lie Abraham, Sugarloaf, and Bigelow Mountains. Cupsuptic Lake and Bald Mountain in Oquossoc are off to the left. Well north of Mooselookmeguntic are West and East Kennebago Mountains. After enjoying these splendid views, drive north as the road drops gradually toward Oquossoc village and pass the entrance to Rangeley Lake State Park at 32 miles, opposite a general store. Park camping is available by reservation or drop-in. You'll cross the Rangeley town line in another half mile. The road follows the shore of Rangeley Lake, visible here and there through the trees, as you drive into Oquossoc at 35½ miles.

Oquossoc offers local shopping, gasoline, eating places, and accommodations, but remains only a small crossroads. It is hard to imagine that the railroad once served this community (you were paralleling the old railroad right-of-way as you drove into town). Haines Landing and the road to Bald Mountain are to the west, or left, as you turn right and east and motor through Mountainview on Routes 4 and 16, headed now for Rangeley. The drive toward Rangeley goes past the road to Wilsons Mills, and carries you over a series of hills with fine views ahead to the town and mountains beyond it. You cross the outlets of Quimby and pretty Dodge Ponds, which flow into Hunter Cove, and soon crest Town Hill with the village ahead.

At forty-two miles you descend into Rangeley village, where we end this journey. This small town seems to have grown in recent years, and offers a choice of accommodations, eating places, and other services, such as guiding and boat rental. For fishing information, visit the Rangeley Region Sport Shop. The Rangeley Region Tourist Office can provide assistance with locating accommodations and services. The town is the hub of extensive hiking trails, with the Appalachian Trail route up Saddleback being one of the most challenging. The town holds a lumberjack competition each year and snowmobile rallies in winter.

Route 6

Augusta-Belgrade Lakes-Augusta

Highway:

Routes 27, 225, 8

Distance:

56½ miles (around loop)

Maine contains hundreds of lakes and ponds, some gathered into tight clusters where the vacationing is good and the scenery grand. The Belgrade Lakes have exerted this kind of appeal for visitors for many years, and the region is full of private camps, children's summer camps, public rental accommodations, boating services, and restaurants. Long Pond, Great Pond, North Pond, East Pond, McGrath Pond, and Ellis Pond constitute the Belgrade "lakes," the latter two being the smaller bodies of water within this multilake aggregation. Surrounded by pine woods and backed by rolling hills, all these lakes have a quiet, quintessentially Maine flavor. The lakes reside in rural country; development in the area has been modest, with none of the big-resort ugliness often common at suc

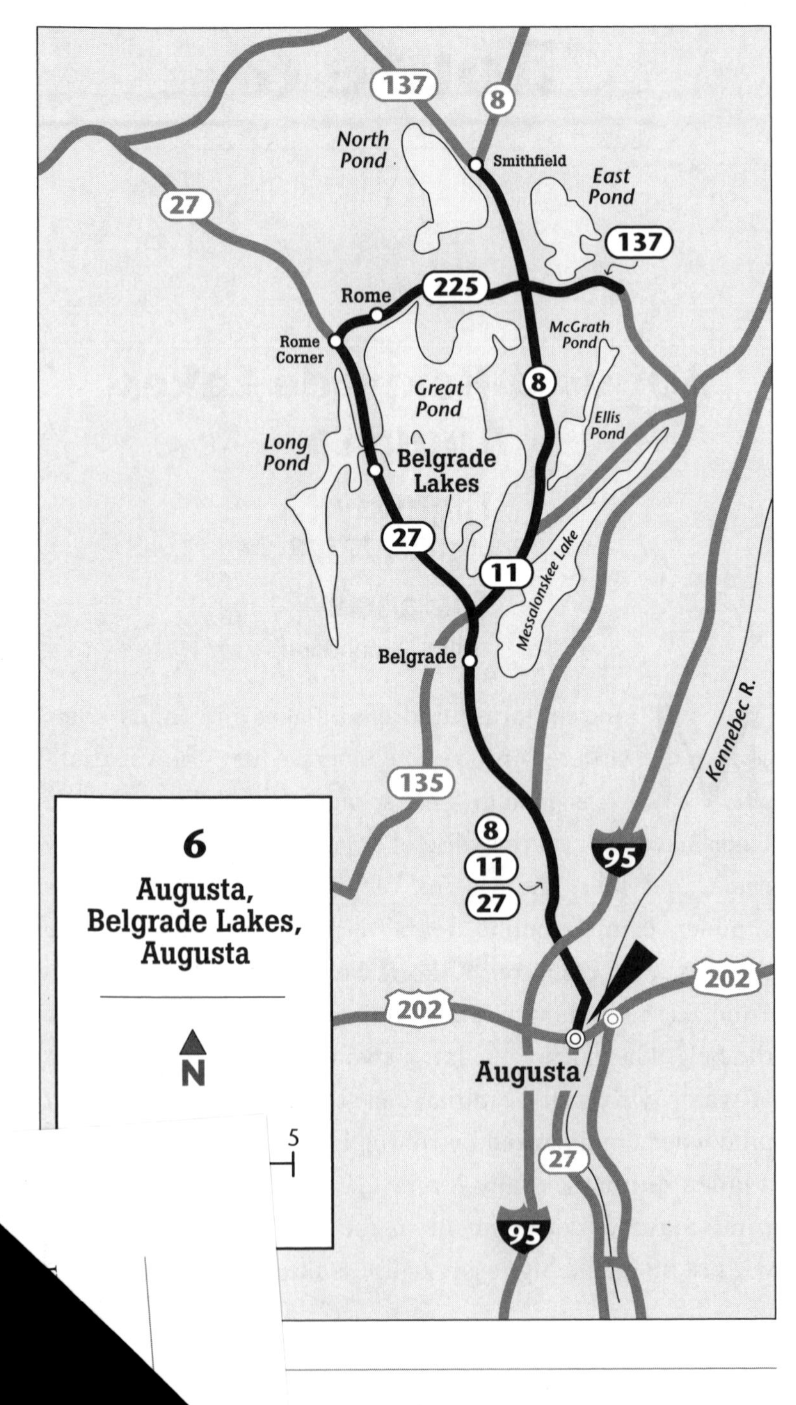
137
8
North Pond
Smithfield
East Pond
27
137
225
Rome
Rome Corner
McGrath Pond
8
Great Pond
Ellis Pond
Long Pond
Belgrade Lakes
27
11
Messalonskee Lake
Belgrade
Kennebec R.
135
6
Augusta, Belgrade Lakes, Augusta
N
5
8
11
27
95
202
202
Augusta
27
95

places elsewhere. A trip through this region offers pleasant views any time of year, with striking foliage in autumn and swimming, boating, camping, and walking in summer.

This drive forms a loop beginning in Augusta, the state capital, running north around the lakes, and back again. Also suggested are a couple of minor diversions that allow you to pull off the loop for a moment to see two of the ponds not on the inner circuit. The trip begins at the West Side Rotary in Augusta, just two blocks north of the Maine State House and the Blaine House, the governor's residence. If you travel on a weekday, you may wish to first visit these buildings and the adjacent Maine State Museum, which features exceptional displays and collections reflecting Maine history, natural science, and culture. The state museum is also open Sunday afternoons. (Call for visiting hours, which may change periodically.)

From the West Side Rotary, go north on Route 27 (State Street), shortly passing the Maine District Court, The Kennebec County Administration Building, Kennebec County Jail, and Kennebec County Superior Court. Continue north on Route 27 as it drops downhill, with views of the spires of St. Augustine's Church ahead, and then winds west and north, passing the entrance to the University of Maine at Augusta campus on your left at 2½ miles. The entrance to the Marketplace at Augusta is on the right at 2¾ miles. Route 27, now Civic Center Drive, then passes the Augusta Civic Center complex on the left. The route goes under Interstate 95, passes the Augusta Business Park to the left and Maine Veterans Memorial Cemetery on the right, and continues out of town toward Sidney. You'll reach the

Sidney town line in 6½ miles. Pass a junction where Route 23 separates from Route 27. Stay on Route 27 through Belgrade Depot at just over ten miles and come immediately to a seasonal travelers' information booth, also on the right. Just beyond, at 10½ miles, is the boat landing area for Messalonskee Lake, with wide views of the marsh and lake. These views continue for a while after you cross pretty Hoyt Brook Stream, which enters the lake here. A small, attractive roadside picnic area is on the left.

Passing Workman Municipal Field at 11½ miles, you arrive at a junction by the Belgrade Post Office, where Route 8 and 11 go right at just over twelve miles. You continue northwest on Route 27 here, passing the Belgrade Municipal Offices at a junction with Route 135. The road runs through fields and more wooded countryside, soon crossing an outflow stream from the Austin Bog. At 15¾ miles, you pass the Narrows Road on your left, which leads to Castle Island and Mount Vernon. This side road (called Castle Island Road on some maps) is worth a few minutes off the main route, as it provides fine north-south views over the Long Pond narrows. Views of the hills to the north appear as Route 27 crests the height-of-land and begins a descent into Belgrade Lakes, passing the entrance to Great Pond Marina (boat rentals) at 16½ miles. Around a bend the route comes into the town of Belgrade.

Small shops, Victorian houses, restaurants, inns, a general store (fuel), and dramatic views across Long Pond characterize the settled district here. A falls connects Long Pond and Great Pond by a water-side park beyond the general store at 17½ miles. Quiet and largely unvisited in winter,

Belgrade Lakes manages to be a bustling, interesting place in high summer.

Route 27 runs up the hill at the end of the shopping district and skirts Long Pond, with occasional water views through the trees. You head away from the lake by Tracy Cove at 19½ miles and continue northward, cresting a hill and arriving at a junction with Route 225. Turn right here at signs to Rome and Oakland by the old Grange Hall. Follow Route 225 eastward as it dips and winds through pretty, heavily forested countryside bordered by old stone walls. Climbing slightly at twenty-two miles, you reach a gravel turnout and, just beyond it, a green trail sign at the head of the path to Mount Philip. (See the author's *50 Hikes in Southern and Coastal Maine* [Backcountry Publications] for a description of this easy hike.) Route 225 then dips sharply to the east through more sparsely settled country and occasional farms. After mile 23, you top a rise and emerge in rolling, open fields as you proceed northeastward. The road soon reaches the Smithfield town line at 25¾ miles, and enters Somerset County. Here you cross Great Meadow Stream and come to a T with Routes 8 and 137.

Drive left and north now on Route 8 for a three-mile run up to the community of Smithfield. The road climbs through fields and old farms, soon coming into the settled area of Smithfield. Grand views to the left emerge over North Pond, the northernmost of the Belgrade Lakes, and to the hills beyond. Follow this road past Sunset Camps, which lie on the lakeshore, and stop at the Y junction of Routes 137 and 8 at a store (food, fuel) at 29¾ miles. (In swimming season, guests can use Sunset Camps' beach for a small fee.) Reverse direction here and return south to the junction of Routes 225 and 8, enjoying more views of North Pond as you go south.

Go through the intersection with Route 225 and, in a hundred feet, go left on Route 137. Drive eastward here for a short run to the southwest corner of East Pond. Pass the entrance to Camp Matoaka on the left and cross the Oakland town line at 33¾ miles. Slow for limited views of East Pond's southeast corner as you round a bend and look left from a gravel shoulder. Brush has grown up along the shore, but you can see up East Pond in the direction of Libby Point and Brickett Point.

Make a U-turn on this gravel shoulder, using care, and retrace your route to the junction with Route 8. Turn left on Route 8 at just over thirty-five miles and drive south. The road widens for a moment as you proceed toward North Belgrade in pretty, mixed-growth forest. At thirty-six miles, you cross the Belgrade town line again and pass a side road, Old Route 8. The road begins to climb Howland Hill at thirty-seven miles and gradually follows a ridge, going by McGrath Pond Road on the left at 38½ miles. (If you wish, a drive of about 2½ miles down this road will bring you to views of McGrath Pond from its north end.) Up on this ridge, you are really heading south between two of the Belgrade Lakes: McGrath Pond below and to the east, and Great Pond below and to the west. Neither is visible at this point.

You drive next past the Belgrade Community Center at roughly thirty-nine miles, and Tukey Brothers lumber mill, a usually busy warren of stacked trees, milled lumber, logging trucks, and sawdust. Continuing south past the Spaulding

Point Road (called Horse Point Road on some maps), you go through a settled area, with Ellis Pond hidden in the trees to the left. Climbing onto another ridge, the road levels off by two nice old farms at a junction with Route 11 at 41½ miles. Pause at this intersection, as there are excellent views to the upper reaches of Messalonskee Lake across the road here. More lake views to the east are visible from time to time as you roll along southward at 42½ miles.

You drive through more open fields at 43¾ miles, staying on the ridge. The road soon dips at a junction with Route 135, and you press on southward on Route 8 and 11. At just under forty-five miles, you rejoin Route 27, and bear left at the Belgrade Post Office, continuing southward for the return to Augusta.

You may find this just as rewarding a drive in winter, when, with the leaves gone, views to the lakes are more open, and rolling fields and hills are covered with bright, glistening snow.

Route 7

Damariscotta to South Bristol, the Gut, and Rutherford Island

Highway:

Route 129

Distance:

28½ miles (round trip)

This meander to the sea begins in Damariscotta, one of Maine's most inviting villages, on the bank of the river of the same name. The village is approached from north or south on U.S. Route 1. Damariscotta has an inviting traditional main street with shops, restaurants, bookstores, and other amenities. Plan to pause here for lunch at one of the several eateries and enjoy browsing at Maine Coast Bookshop and Café on Main Street.

Begin this pretty drive down one of the midcoast's narrowest peninsulas by turning south off Main Street onto Route 129 (Bristol Road). The turn is made on the rise at the east end of the shopping district, by the old fire station. Follow ME 129 south and southeast as it roams through a district of pretty homes and passes Cottage Point with river

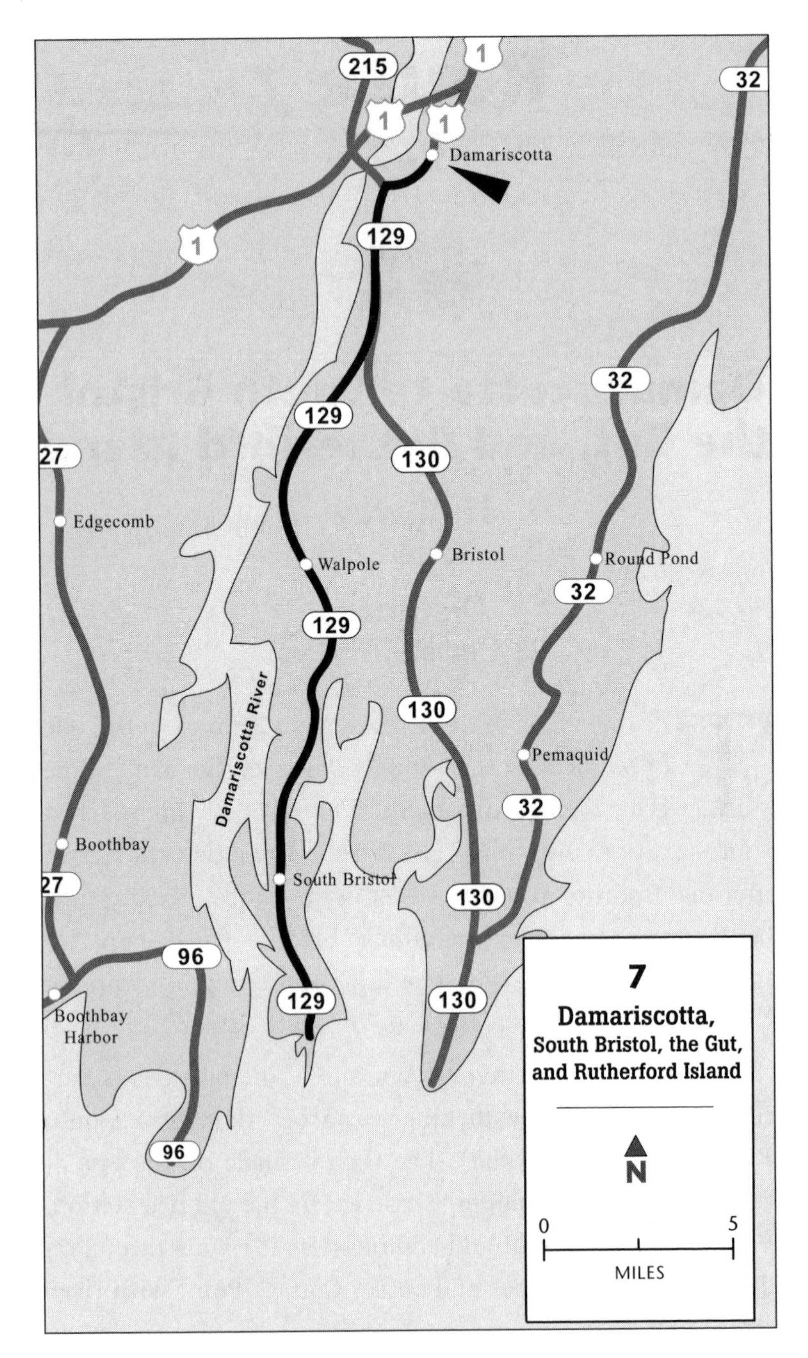
215
1
32
1
1
Damariscotta
1
129
32
129
27
130
Edgecomb
Bristol
Walpole
Round Pond
32
129
Damariscotta River
130
Pemaquid
32
Boothbay
South Bristol
27
130
96
129
130
Boothbay
Harbor
96
7
Damariscotta,
South Bristol, the Gut,
and Rutherford Island
N
0
5
MILES

views to the west. The Down Easter Inn is passed on the left at mile one, and there are occasional artist and antique galleries along here, too, worth visiting in season.

Drive next through a corridor of pleasant old Capes and farmhouses, a reminder of the flavor of this place in earlier days, backed to the west with views of the Damariscotta River. Moving through more open countryside at just under three miles, you bear right and southwest on ME 129, known as the Walpole Road. This is ledgy country, layers of reddish sedimentary rock bordering both sides of the road for some distance. Rock of this type serves as a reminder that millions of years ago, this area lay under the sea. At 3.6 miles, the old Walpole Meetinghouse is passed on the left. Going farther southwest and west, the road descends amidst white pine and deciduous forest, where you shortly come upon the Brannon Bunker Inn at 4.5 miles.

The road pulls more to the south at 5.2 miles as you reach the point where this finger of land begins to narrow considerably, and you pass the roadside marker for the Walpole Woods reservation at 5.6 miles. Going by the diminutive Walpole Post Office and Walpole Union Chapel, you follow 129 around to the southeast and through a series of broad curves. This is sparsely settled country, and, though you can't see it yet behind the screen of trees, the Johns River is very close. At 8 miles a roadside marker indicates the way to the nearby Harrington House Museum.

Stone walls border the road as it narrows at 9 miles and passes more old farm structures, pastures, and orchards. Cresting a height-of-land, you roll by a couple of farms with distinctive barns. The road jogs westward at 9.7 miles, descending southward again, and entering a more built-up area where some houses sport stacks of lobster traps stacked high in their yards. In winter, Eastporters, Novi boats, and their kin lie becalmed in these same yards, waiting for the next season. At 10.8 miles, the Plummer Point Preserve is marked to the right.

As the point of land narrows, 129 winds, climbs, dips, and turns to stay on the high ground. This is likely to have been the route of a rough cart track in days before the automobile. Pass the Hopscotch Ice Museum and the Tracy Shore Preserve at 11.7 miles. You'll see the Rutherford Library and then the South Bristol School at 12.4 miles. Just beyond, you slow to enter South Bristol village, soon noting the Gamage shipyard on the right, once one of Maine's premier yacht builders. Descending, you see a small harbor on your left, and then pass Osier's Wharf and several utility buildings as the road narrows for the bridge over the Gut. The local lobster fleet, a seiner or two, and other workboats lay in the small harbor to the left.

The Gut, a narrow passage with a draw bridge, allows boaters from the Johns and Pemaquid Rivers to move west and return without having to go around Rutherford Island when they head to Linekin Bay and Boothbay. In summer, you may have a wait here, as boat traffic can be heavy and the bridge is often raised. Not a bit like the traffic jams you may be used to.

Crossing the Gut onto Rutherford Island, you wind through more of South Bristol where there are fine views of the lower Damariscotta to the right. 129 pulls sharply left and then right again, passing the post office at 12.2 miles.

You next go by Bittersweet Landing Boatyard, and soon come to excellent views of Christmas Cove on your right. The Inn at Christmas Cove is gained by Coveside Road here. Scattered views east to Birch and Hay Islands appear on the left and to the mouth of the Damariscotta to the west and right as you now enter the very narrow neck of land that is the terminus of this drive.

Grand open-ocean views are seen at 14.1 miles and there are further views east as you pass through a cluster of old waterside homes. Cresting a rise at a dead-end sign, you bear right and descend slightly to a sandy parking area where there are superb views over the mouth of the Damariscotta and out to Inner Heron Island, and, well beyond it in the Gulf of Maine, to Thrumcap. Off to the west lies Linekin Neck. Pause here and relax, enjoying the perspective over open water. When you're ready, head north, following 129 back along the same route you travelled earlier for your return to Damariscotta village.

Route 8

Gardiner to Bath

Highway:

Routes 24, 197, 128, U.S. Route 1

Distance:

27 miles (one way)

Of the Maine routes that keep company with great rivers, this is one of the best. There are plenty of water views along this drive from the attractive central Maine river town of Gardiner southward. We'll travel to Bath, one of Maine's great maritime cities, former home of America's shipbuilding industry during the heady, early days of the Republic. Between points, we'll explore pretty rural countryside along the bank of the Kennebec, in lands closely tied to early settlement in northern New England.

Begin in Gardiner, a few miles south of Augusta. From the lights in the downtown Gardiner shopping district, drive south on Route 24, shortly passing an old railroad yard. Soon, views open up to the Kennebec on your left. Watch for a handful of half-submerged rocks at low water, often

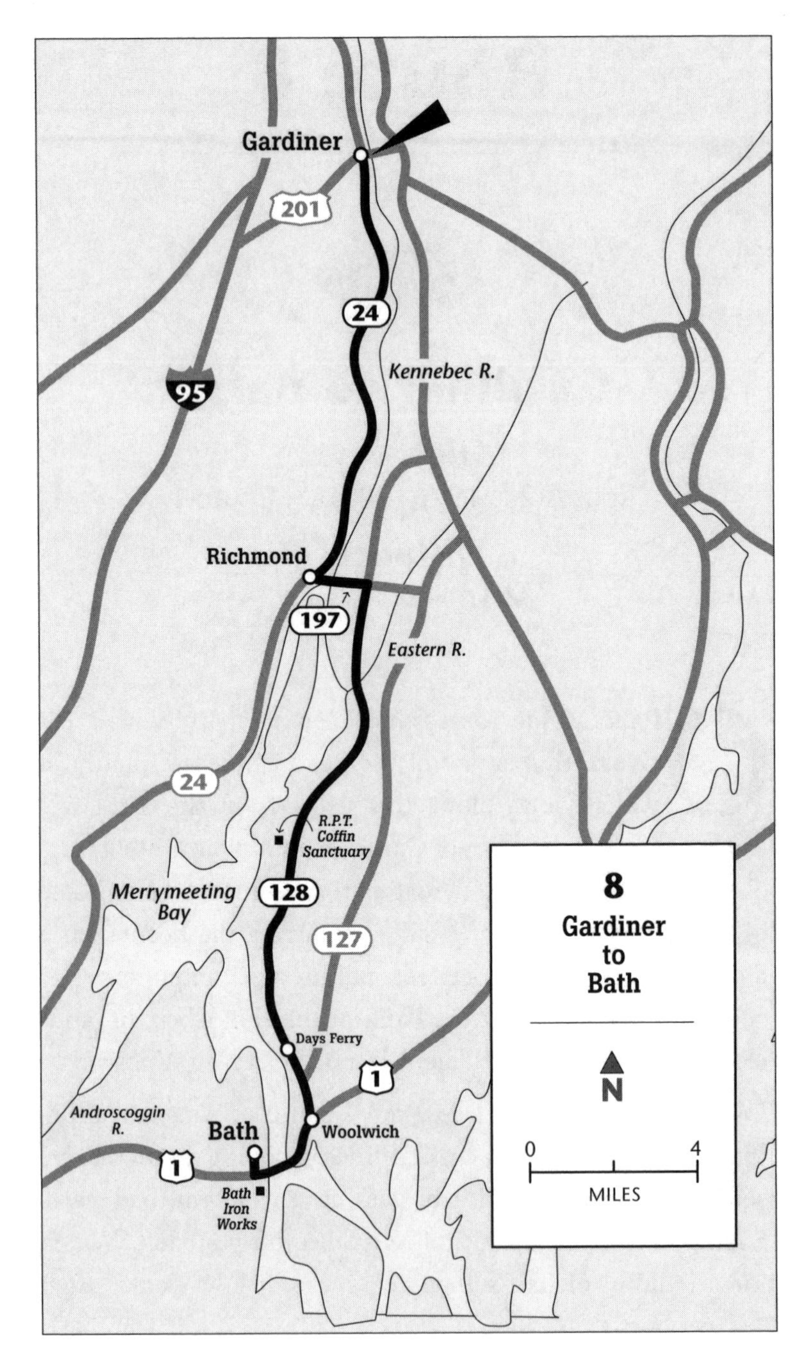
Gardiner
201
24
Kennebec R.
95
Richmond
197
Eastern R.
24
R.P.T.
Coffin
Sanctuary
Merrymeeting
Bay
128
127
Days Ferry
1
Androscoggin
R.
Bath
Woolwich
1
Bath
Iron
Works
8
Gardiner
to
Bath
N
0
4
MILES

occupied in the warm months by cormorants. Look for some excellent views, too, along the Kennebec as the road and railway parallel the riverbank while you proceed southward. The town of Randolph lies across the river. An interesting, castellated house rests on a bluff above a field to the right, 1⅓ miles south of Gardiner.

The Kennebec has figured strongly in Maine's economic growth since the earliest days of settlement. The river has been a major artery of commerce and exploration, and it has been a watery highway for pulp logs coming down-country. It has played a significant role in U.S. military history as well. This section of the Kennebec once was home to a unique Maine industry, the cutting of river ice for transport to large eastern cities. Beginning about 1860, crews cut river ice, packed it in sawdust, and sent it downriver and on to such places as Boston, New York, and Philadelphia. Millions of tons of packed river ice moved by boat toward these urban centers in the busiest years, but the ice industry ended when refrigeration became available toward the turn of the century.

A densely wooded shore contains the east side of the river as you drive on and gradually pull away from the water for a while at a bit over three miles, entering South Gardiner. Route 24, known as River Avenue, runs through this little town and continues south. Pass the diminutive South Gardiner Post Office at 4½ miles. Just beyond, at the south end of town, leave Route 24 for a moment, turning left onto Riverview Drive by the Riverview Congregational Church. Follow this quiet local street as it continues along the Kennebec at close quarters. There are striking views downriver. This street, host to some fine old houses, soon connects again with Route 24, where you turn left and southward once more.

Continuing south, you drive over a hill with more river and island views, then through the Chestnut Hill area at six miles. A strip of islands is visible in the river to your left as you cross the Sagadahoc County line. A pretty, winding, hilly ride characterizes the next several miles of countryside, which are dotted with farms and attractive mixed-growth woodlands. The road next holds to a high rib of land, and more river outlooks appear from time to time. Forsythia borders isolated houses in early spring, and horses idle in a sloping roadside pasture at 9¼ miles.

At eleven miles, the road descends toward Richmond to the southwest. At 11½ miles, you make an abrupt left turn down a hillside street by a large Victorian house. Follow this street for a few hundred yards, then make another left on Route 197. In seconds, you cross the Richmond bridge over the now broad Kennebec. This striking bridge is the first major river crossing south of Gardiner. It swings open on demand to admit considerable summer boat traffic upriver. In winter, bald eagles often are seen on the ice, looking for carrion and open water.

Once across the river, having driven 12½ miles, you shortly bear right on Route 128 (River Road) at a pine grove and cemetery. Pass the old brick Dresden Historical Society building on your right. The structure, on the National Register of Historic Places, is open for viewing at posted hours. Soon back in open, rolling country, you drive on southward, passing the entrance to Popp Farm, a haven for strawberry lovers in summer. Around the bend, you'll

The broad expanse of the tidal Kennebec at Days Ferry

drive through the working fields of Goranson Farm, Carlson Farms, and the orchards of Green Point Farm. Truly excellent fruit and produce are sold from farm stands along here in summer and autumn. Here you cross a bridge offering beautiful downriver views to the meandering Kennebec.

More scenic, winding, hill-and-dale driving takes you through farm country again. In some cases, the road literally goes through former farmyards, between house and barn. Slow down, please. Like so many Maine backcountry lanes, this road was established in the days of the horse and buggy, when trotting through someone's yard seemed acceptably neighborlike. At 17½ miles, by a striking brick farmhouse, expect good views west to the Kennebec. In minutes you drive into Woolwich from Dresden.

Downstream on the Kennebec River

At nearly nineteen miles, after passing Thwing Road on the right, you come to the Robert P. Tristram Coffin Wildflower Reservation in dense pine woods to your right. The reservation, owned by the New England Wildflower Society's Maine Chapter, is home to many species of wild plants, flowers, and shrubs. An attractive walking path connects with the riverbank. Look for small signs and a box attached to a tree (visible from the road if you go slowly) just into the woods. A walk here provides some exercise and a very rewarding break in your drive.

Only yards beyond the reservation, your route bends sharply to the left past Chopps Point Road, descends to a gully, rises to pass the North Woolwich Church, and meanders through an open corridor crossed by power lines near Chopps Cross Road. You next drive southeast through more farm country with some architecturally distinguished old houses, and then wind your way into the fine old village of Days Ferry at twenty-three miles.

Days Ferry is characterized by well-kept houses of the Colonial and Federal period, all perched on a hillside above the Kennebec. To the right, if you look hard enough, you'll see approximately where the ferry crossing lay in former years. Downriver are views of Bath's Sagadahoc Bridge, backed by the great cranes of Bath Iron Works. A further short and very winding drive brings you, at twenty-four miles, to the junction of Route 127 (Middle Road), where you bear right and descend in a few miles to another junction, this time with U.S. Route 1 (26 miles).

This is one of those rare times we'll direct you along U.S .Route 1, and here only to bear right (south) and across the Sagadahoc Bridge into Bath. A majestic view of Bath Iron Works (left) and the city of Bath is before you as you cross the half-mile-wide Kennebec. Leave U.S. Route 1 as soon as you cross the river and keep right onto Bath's Front Street, where this route ends (27 miles).

Bath still boasts hilltop streets lined with great houses, a legacy of the days when the city was the center of Kennebec shipbuilding and trade, and a significant influence on regional politics. Deeded by Indians and first incorporated in 1781, the city became a major outpost of the great proprietors, largely Massachusetts-based, who controlled the vast territory of Maine through a series of royal grants. Besides an attractive downtown area, there are many historic sights in Bath, foremost among them the Maine Maritime Museum, a fine window on the city's unique connection with shipbuilding and oceangoing commerce. The museum is now lodged in new facilities on the bank of the Kennebec. Visiting schooners, various small-boat building projects, and other exhibits make this one of the most important displays of its kind in New England.

Route 9

Woolwich to Georgetown and Reid State Park

Highway:

Route 127, Sequinland Road, park roads

Distance:

15 miles (one way)

This short, scenic drive wends its way down a finger of coastal land through woodlands and marsh to two of Maine's most spectacular ocean beaches in Reid State Park, itself one of Maine's most striking coastal reservations. Other than very limited settlement in Arrowsic and Georgetown, this road traverses a little-developed area and proceeds to progressively wooded country as it descends to the Atlantic. Reid State Park, with its unique shore and ocean interface, offers a dramatic place to walk at any time of year, to snowshoe and ski cross-country in winter, and to swim and picnic in summer.

To make this drive, leave U.S. Route 1 at the east end of the Sagadahoc Bridge connecting Bath and Woolwich, and head south on Route 127. Access to Route 127 can be gained

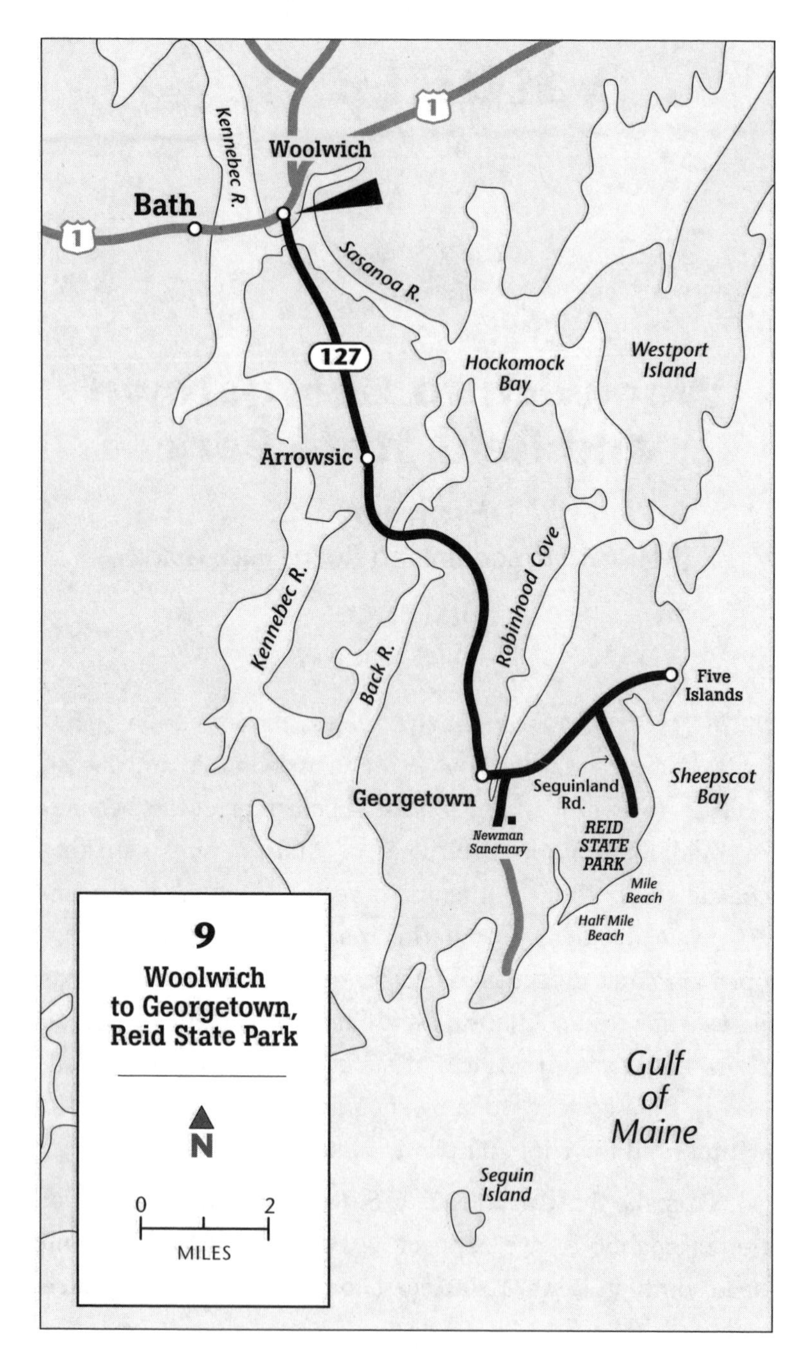
Woolwich
Bath
Kennebec R.
Sasanoa R.
127
Hockomock Bay
Westport Island
Arrowsic
Robinhood Cove
Kennebec R.
Back R.
Five Islands
Georgetown
Seguinland Rd.
Sheepscot Bay
Newman Sanctuary
REID STATE PARK
Mile Beach
Half Mile Beach
9
Woolwich to Georgetown, Reid State Park
N
0
2
MILES
Gulf of Maine
Seguin Island

from either north- or southbound lanes; watch for signs. The route immediately crosses a high bridge over waters connecting the Sasanoa River and the Kennebec River to the west. (When crossing the bridge, note the large nest of an osprey on the top girders of the structure. Ospreys have been nesting on the bridge for several summers now.)

Steeples, chimneys, and the rooftops of old Federals in Bath

Westward views over the Kennebec to Bath Iron Works appear here, and you may wish to pull off the road onto the gravel shoulder at the south end of the bridge to take in these east-west views. Bath Iron Works is the latest in a long line of shipbuilding enterprises here on the Kennebec. Bath was once the world capital of shipbuilding in the golden age of wooden ships. Today, BIW builds Aegis-Class Guided Missile Destroyers.

Continue southward on Route 127, crossing a marshy area with leftward views to Hanson Bay and the Sasanoa River. Red-tailed and northern harrier hawks may be seen circling over this marsh, particularly in autumn. The road rises southward and widens, cuts through some hillside deposits of shale, and comes, at two miles, to the Arrowsic Town Hall (1850). You drive through another marsh in moments, with water views on the west side toward Fiddler

Reach in the Kennebec. Then pass the diminutive Arrowsic Fire Department at 3⅓ miles, and next go by pretty Sewell Pond on your left. The road winds southwest and south in mixed-growth forest dominated by stands of white pine and red oak.

At four miles the road heads more eastward and enters another marsh with good views to the right. Acres of cattails wave in low ground to both sides of the road. You crest a ledgy rise, cross Old Stage Road at 4½ miles, and drop to more marsh views again. At five miles you go over a bridge above the scenic Back River, with excellent outlooks north and south. There is a small turnout for parking at the south end of the bridge (use caution). Beyond the bridge, you drive more southeasterly and south in Georgetown, passing the road to Robinhood Cove at 8¾ miles. It is not immediately noticeable to the driver, but Arrowsic and Georgetown are separate islands divided from each other by the Back River. You left the mainland when you crossed the bridge at Woolwich. You have been island-hopping ever since.

The route hugs a high ridge, passes an old cemetery at seven miles, and continues up and down, winding southward in sparsely settled countryside. Go through some S curves at just over eight miles, and shortly you come to the bend in the road that is Georgetown. Pass Georgetown Pottery studios on the right at 8⅔ miles, the country store, and the fire department, and stay left on Route 127 at the curve. The road drops quickly eastward here in a settled area to the tiny Historical Society on another bend in the road, where a bridge takes you over the southern tip of Robinhood Cove at just over nine miles. Quiet Georgetown

Robinhood Cove at the bend in the road: Georgetown

is a community intimately tied to the early Colonial settlement of Maine, and boasted 1,700 settlers at the onset of the American Revolution.

Once across the bridge, watch immediately on the right for a gravel road that provides entry to the Josephine Newman Sanctuary, a fine natural reservation owned by the Maine Audubon Society. The 119-acre former farmstead is host to a network of easy walking trails connecting the two arms of Robinhood Cove that border it on the east and west. The preserve lands are very attractive and may be visited year-round. (For trail descriptions of the Newman Sanctuary, consult the author's *Walking the New England Coast* [Down East Books].) Around the bend beyond the preserve you cross another bridge over Robinhood Cove.

The road climbs sharply northward, then works its way eastward, goes over two ridges, and drops down again to a junction with Seguinland Road, where you leave Five Islands Road and bear right. Watch for prominent signs indicating Reid State Park. You pass the first of several little ponds on the right, attractive winter and summer. Going more southward, the road passes an oceanside inn and then winds past another marshy pond bordered by dri-ki in woods increasingly dominated by jack pines and other conifers. A walking and cross-country ski trail comes out to this spot from the main parklands. At 12¾ miles, after a final broad bend, the road arrives at the main gate of Reid State Park, which is open to visitors throughout the year. (A small admission charge is levied during the summer months. Season passes can be purchased.)

There are two major headlands at Reid. Once through the gate, keep left and drive first to Griffith Head. This road leads you past a parking area near sand beaches and continues across the backmarsh stream to the main parking area, bathhouse, and limited food service at 13½ miles. From the parking area here, take the short trail to Griffith Head, with spectacular views of One-Mile Beach to the south. You will see three lighthouses from this spot. Far back to the left is Hendricks Head Light, to the northeast is Cuckolds Light, and way down to the south is distinctive Seguin Light, the highest lighthouse on America's east coast. A fourth lighthouse, Ram Island Light, is behind Cuckolds but cannot be seen from here except during exceptionally clear weather.

When you've had ample time to explore the rocks and shore, drive back to the main gate and turn left at signs indicating Todds Point, going left again at 13¾ miles on the road to the point. Good views over the backmarsh toward Seguin open soon and continue through trees to the left. A tremendous variety of birdlife frequents these woods and the backmarsh. Deer are plentiful. Cresting a small hill, you drop to a wider point in the marsh. Hawks and eagles are often overhead, as are sea crows and a wide variety of shorebirds. A tidal stream goes under the roadway. Dense bayberry hedges line both sides of the right-of-way.

Climbing another rise, the road winds to the parking lot at Todds Point, where you'll find a bathhouse and limited food-service facilities at just over fifteen miles. Immediately offshore are the rock ledges known as the Three Sisters. You may spot seals cavorting in the water here. Seguin Island lies, as before, to the south. To the right, behind the dunes, is Half-Mile Beach, another beautiful, sandy strand that runs westward to the inlet of the Little River. This river is tidal and absorbs major influxes of ocean water during storms. I have found beached whales here after bad weather in winter. Protected bird species such as the least tern nest in the dunes in late spring. Walkers should keep away from the dunes, which are fragile. Picnic tables are available at both Griffith Head and Todds Point in season.

The Todds Point section of this road is closed to driving in winter, but is open to walkers. Consult with wardens at the main gate in season for trail directions and other park features.

On leaving the park, you may simply follow Seguinland Road and Route 127 northward to U.S. Route 1. However, if you have time, an additional short ride will garner further excellent water views. When you come back to the intersection with Five Islands Road, keep right and follow this road for a short distance as it winds through attractive country to Harmon Harbor and Five Islands. The fine views are well worth the short detour.

Route 10

Coopers Mills–Whitefield–Head Tide–Newcastle–Dodge Point

Highway:
Routes 218, 194, 215, River Road

Distance:
25 miles (one way)

Here is an attractive backroads journey starting between Augusta and Rockland that works its way south and east to Newcastle and Damariscotta, and on to the State of Maine's beautiful Dodge Point Reservation on the Damariscotta River. This trip makes its way through rural farm country, past lakes and streams, and over rolling hills, and winds up in a historic area of the midcoast. As with so many of the drives in this book, this route is one that very few travelers from elsewhere see, even though it crosses under, at one point, overbusy U.S. Route 1 and is near a number of popular tourist destinations.

Begin this journey at the junction of Routes 17 and 218 in Coopers Mills, about twelve miles east of Augusta. The intersection is marked, but watch carefully, and go southwest on Route 218, where you are immediately in a

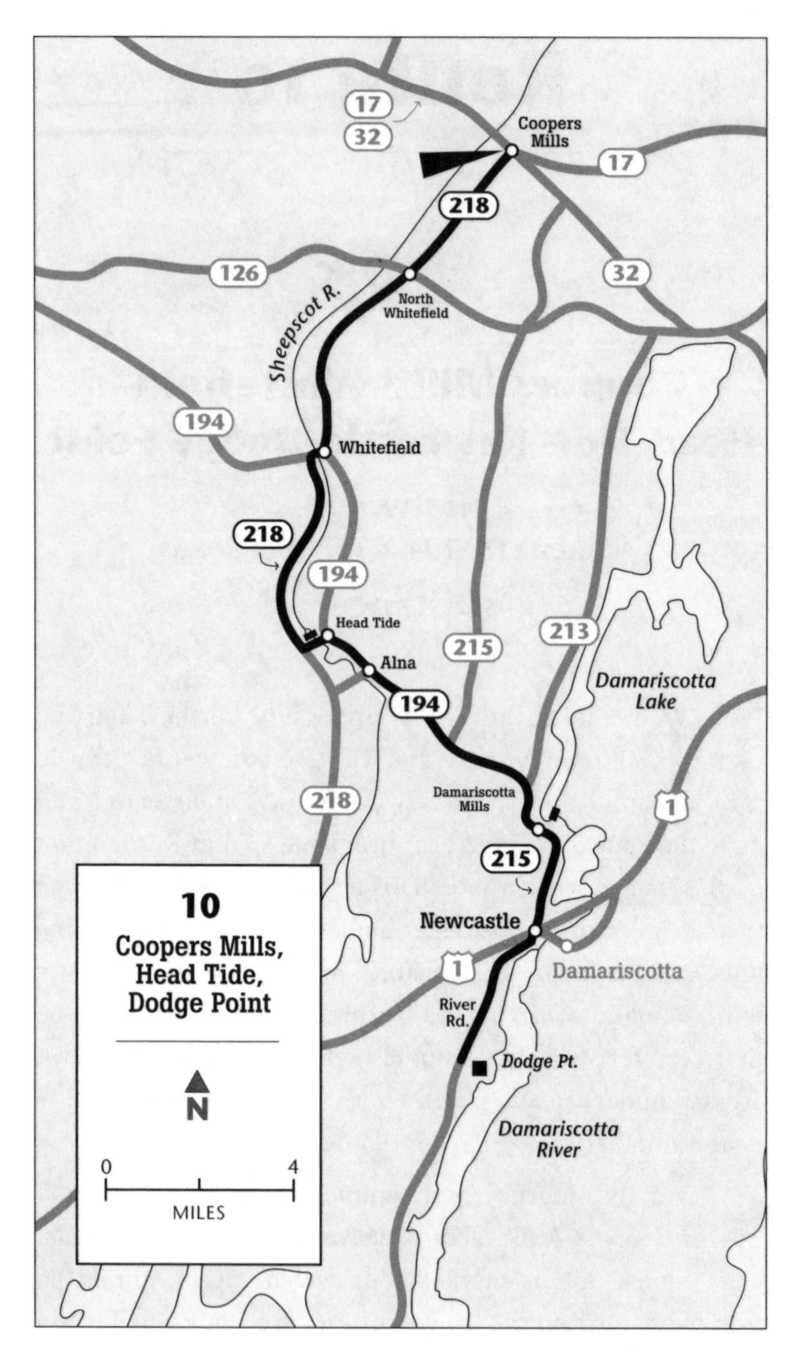

17
32
Coopers Mills
17
218
126
32
Sheepscot R.
North Whitefield
194
Whitefield
218
194
Head Tide
Alna
215
213
194
Damariscotta Lake
218
Damariscotta Mills
1
215
10
Coopers Mills, Head Tide, Dodge Point
N
0
4
MILES
Newcastle
1
Damariscotta
River Rd.
Dodge Pt.
Damariscotta River

neighborhood of pleasant old houses and barns. You rise onto a rib of land surrounded by pastures with excellent views westward over old stone walls and grazing cows. Big hardrock maples line the roadside, with occasional limited views off to the west again. At 2½ miles the road opens out in fields and paddocks, with a marsh and pond visible to the left, the westernmost flowage of Clary Lake. On the right is an old mill. Winding more to the southeast, you come to a T with Route 126 in North Whitefield at just over three miles. Bear left and east here where Routes 218 and 126 run together. After one hundred yards, bear right and south again on Route 218 as the roads separate.

Your route now goes by an old farm with a silo and dips and winds southward in broad fields of goldenrod. Wending more southwestward, you go through pretty, undulating country, farmhouses in fields backed by woods, and occasional farther views to westward. Farms across the vale are visible in the distance. Continuing down the ridge in pine and oak growth you pass the entrance to Maine Helicopters at nearly five miles.

Attractive barns and old houses are situated along the road at 5½ miles. It is increasingly rare to drive a Maine road and see undisturbed old farms and traditional architecture like this. With every year, there are fewer such roads. Sheep and goats are raised on farms hereabouts, and you come to a section at over six miles with pasture on both sides of the road where sheep are often grazing. You will pass a farmhouse that makes goat cheese for sale. Open fields nearby are dotted with rolled-up biscuits of hay.

After cresting another ridge above a junction with Route 194, you enter a settled area—the little village of Whitefield.

Pass Head Tide Road and cross a bridge over the Sheepscot River. Go left now on Route 218 (Wiscasset Road) at a junction. Drive south by more pasture and an old cemetery at 8¼ miles. Here you'll see more open, rolling countryside with cattle in fields and a small farm pond. The route runs up and down several ridges and goes under power lines at nearly ten miles. The road enters clearings at just under eleven miles by a broad, flat blueberry field and passes Thayer Road, continuing southeast.

Going under that power line again, you drop east and southeast, and soon go left off Route 218 at 12¼ miles, taking a little connector road into Head Tide village. Pass the dam over the Sheepscot here on the bend (parking available), and then go over the Sheepscot, arriving amid a cluster of serene old buildings that constitute Head Tide village. The Sheepscot has its charms here, particularly in spring, and it is not hard to see why early settlers favored this place. Below here the Sheepscot is tidal, with an unusual reversing falls in Sheepscot village downstream. Some of the fine old houses associated with this early settlement still perch on the bend in the road as you pass.

You follow the Sheepscot eastward for a bit on Route 194, but the river soon turns away southward. Continuing out of town on Route 194 you pass more of the settlement and come to open fields full of goldenrod. Going over a rise at thirteen miles, the river comes back to the road below and to the right. You follow it to the east, rolling past the Newcastle-Alna Baptist Church, with its simple, castellated steeple, toward an intersection with Dock Road in Alna, by the town offices on your right. Some excellent Federal-style houses are nearly in the road here. One can see they were built in the days when this road was merely a narrow, grassy cart track.

The road dips sharply and pulls left and right on a hill, crossing the Newcastle town line at 14⅓ miles. Stone walls border the right-of-way, and the heavy woods press in. You descend sharply into a hollow, cross a stream, round the bend by a farm, and then pull northeast. In a short distance you arrive at a junction with Route 215. You go right and east on Route 215 in more winding, up-and-down terrain. Passing under more power lines in wooded, marshy countryside, watch at just under seventeen miles for an opening, where views left to this power line disclose a large osprey nest, usually occupied from year to year in the warmer months. The nest is up on the power poles.

Pass a junction with Route 213, staying right on Route 215 in still more farm country marked by pastures, old barns, and, sometimes, spans of workhorses in the fields to the right in season. Pass West Hamlet Road at 19½ miles by another farmhouse. The route drops leftward and down into a slump and is soon by the southern tip of Damariscotta Lake. In recent years, a pair of bald eagles has nested here pretty reliably in tall pines on the spit of land jutting into the lake. Rounding a bend, you are in the attractive, small settlement of Damariscotta Mills. Follow Route 215 past the milldam through town (bed-and-breakfast accommodations) and down to Bayview Road, where you go right.

Still on Route 215 and now going south, you have fine views of the mill pond and, over the railroad line, Salt Bay, at the head of the Damariscotta River. Crossing the railroad tracks, you proceed toward Newcastle center at 20¼ miles.

Expansive views over Salt Bay appear to the left as you come into Newcastle's settled area. Pass Faith Baptist Church, the U.S. Post Office, and some stores, and go under U.S. Route 1. You arrive at the junction of Route 215 and US Route 1B, diagonally opposite the Second Congregational Church.

Go straight through this intersection, pass the church, and take a left on River Road at an interchange by the Harborview Inn. There are good views of Damariscotta Harbor and the river on your left as you proceed through a neighborhood of old homes, bed-and-breakfast establishments, and inns at 21½ miles. Continue southward out River Road, going by the Town of Newcastle Offices at $22\frac{1}{3}$ miles. Stay left on River Road at an intersection where U.S. Route 1B goes right at $22\frac{2}{3}$ miles. Pass some old orchards on the ridge, with occasional water views to the Damariscotta River to the left. A lovely stone wall follows the road to the right as you travel by a series of attractive period homes. More stone walls appear as you continue southward, pass Perkins Point Road, and arrive, in just over twenty-five miles, at beautiful Dodge Point State Reservation, where this journey ends.

This Maine Department of Conservation preserve offers superb forest and shore trails along the Damariscotta River and merits a visit at any time of year. After your drive, you'll find this natural area a pleasant spot to stretch your legs and walk within beautiful coastal woodlands. (See the author's *50 Hikes in Southern and Coastal Maine* [Backcountry Publications] for trail descriptions for this preserve.) Food, fuel, and accommodations are available in Newcastle and across the bridge in Damariscotta.

Route 11

Belfast–Lincolnville Center–Searsmont–Liberty

Highway:
Routes 52, 173, 220

Distance:
26½ miles (one way)

Here is a fine afternoon drive through rolling, back-of-the-midcoast hill country, where you'll travel from the appealing waterside city of Belfast to the tiny inland town of Liberty. Midcoast Maine is one of the state's most attractive regions, but too many visitors cling only to the overbusy, narrow coastal strip. Behind the coastal zone, a setting of hillside farms, low mountains, scenic ponds, and quiet villages lies, ready for the visiting. The roads connecting these sights roam over rock ribs and hills, cut across fields of uncut hay, and lumber through sleepy crossroads. Nearly devoid of traffic, roads in this region are reminiscent of the kinds of drives older Mainers remember from their childhood, and that many big-city visitors lamentably have never seen. Here are those same roads today, awaiting the traveler's attention.

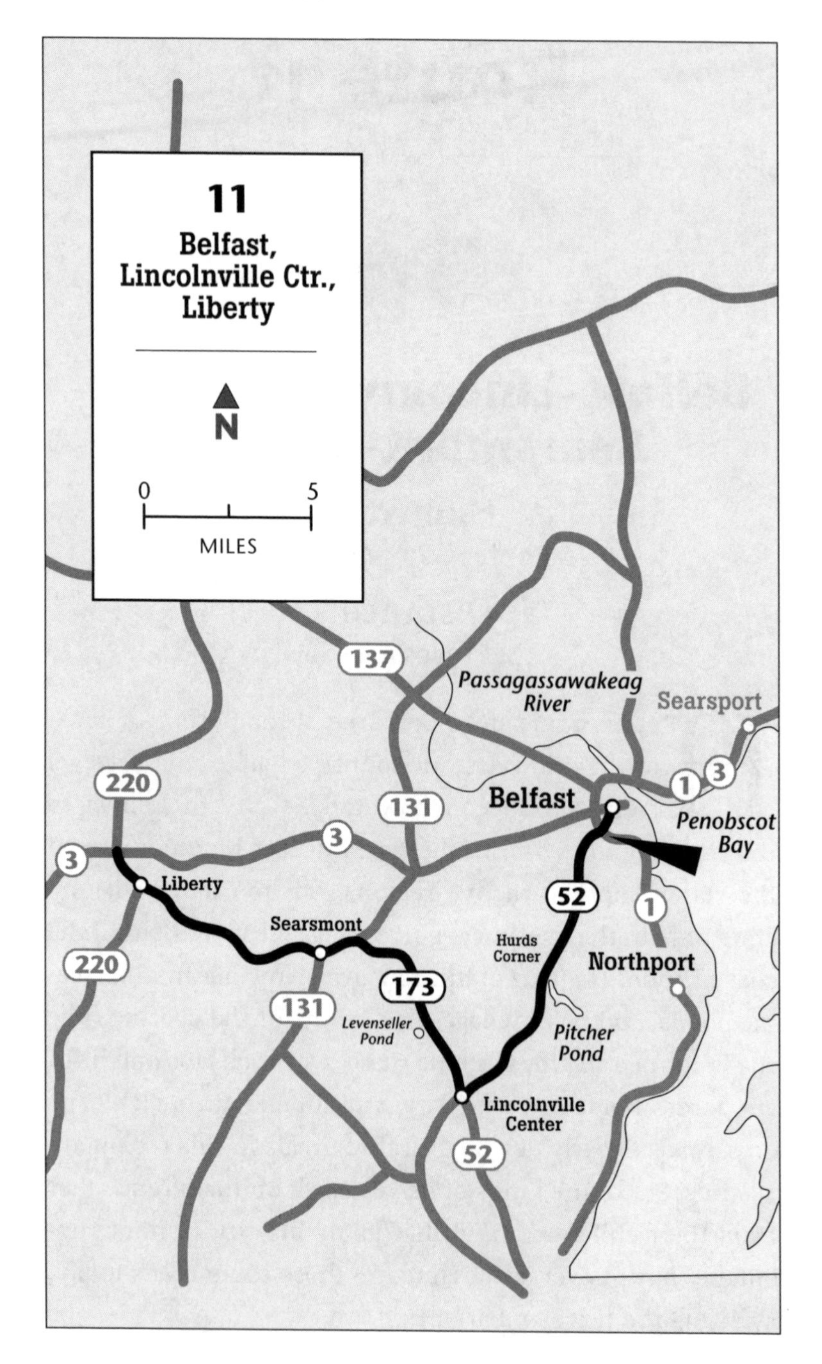
11
Belfast,
Lincolnville Ctr.,
Liberty
N
0
5
MILES
137
Passagassawakeag
River
Searsport
220
131
Belfast
1
3
Penobscot
Bay
3
3
Liberty
52
1
Searsmont
Hurds
Corner
Northport
220
173
131
Levenseller
Pond
Pitcher
Pond
Lincolnville
Center
52

First, Belfast, itself, is worth a visit. Before starting out, spend some hours in this nicely situated old city, with its architecturally distinctive downtown, shops, restaurants, bookstores, railroad terminal, marina, and classic movie theater. Belfast perches on a hillside over a splendid bay fed by the broad Passagassawakeag River. The bay, in turn, dotted with sailing and power craft, leads southeast to the open Atlantic. Belfast is easy to cotton to.

U.S. Route 1 makes a loop around central Belfast. At its intersection with Route 52, turn onto Route 52 (Lincolnville Road) and head southwest. You quickly enter open fields and roll through sparsely settled countryside, passing Edgecomb Road at just over a mile. Climbing south-southwest you reach a junction, where you keep left, ascending farther. Grown-up fields going back to woods, old farms, and roadside stands line the road. Rugged old stone walls and woodlands soon appear on both sides of the highway at 2½ miles. The road climbs farther as it leaves the coastal plain and heads into the hilly terrain typical of this back-country journey.

Working around to the south, you crest another hill and stick to the plateau, with fine rightward views to hills over pasture. Mountain views appear ahead. At 3⅓ miles, you come to a T, where you go right, staying with Route 52 at Prescott Road. You'll pass ruined old farms, bogs, and maples as you roll southwest and climb still another rise.

Outlooks onto the hills to the southeast appear at four miles, and you are driving in more open country. Hardwoods line the road as you climb farther, and more pasture lies to the right at a dairy farm. Going southwesterly through Hurds Corner, you move along a roller-coaster section of

Ducktrap Mountain over Pitcher Pond

road that dips and rises at 5½ miles, as splendid lake and mountain views emerge momentarily over beautiful, narrow Pitcher Pond. Slow for views here.

Route 52 goes along and away from the pond on pretty, rolling ground.

You next descend to the southwest, into a slump, and continue westward by a hill farm at 7⅓ miles. You'll soon pass a column of gaunt white pines. Hills appear to your right at 8¼ miles over a field topped by a windmill, and constantly improving views leftward greet you as you cross Tucker Brook and go through a junction with Slab City Road and Greenacre Road (shown as the Belmont Road on some maps). Going around to the south on Belfast Road (Route 52), the route runs through fields, with superb mountain views now from east to southwest. The road curves to the southwest, and the mountain views just keep getting better from your high vantage point on this ridge-bound highway. You pass Tranquility Grange at 9¾ miles.

Dipping south again, with more hillside outlooks, the road crosses a stream before its junction with Route 173 at 10½ miles, in the little valley crossroads of Lincolnville Center. Here you will turn right and drive northwest on Route 173. Meadows and woods rife with goldenrod line a gully as you next climb a hill in open pasture, go past older houses on the hilltop, and reenter the woods northward with hill views ahead. At 11½ miles the road works northwest on more up-and-down terrain, passes more pasture, and climbs steadily. Pretty Levenseller Pond lies to the left at 12½ miles, where loons (*Gavia immer*) are often sighted. The road stays with the pond here for some distance and then pulls away upward to the north once more. At 13¼ miles, you pass a blueberry field on the right and have glimpses westward into the distance through openings in the trees. Although it has not been noticeable until now, you are quite high on the side of Levenseller Mountain.

You drop northward at 14½ miles in stands of red oaks before fields appear with mountain views. Stone walls line the road as you head northwest in country with few houses, arriving at a T, where you bear left on Route 173 at Bickfords Corner by a stop sign after 15¾ miles. Run due west now and drive straight through rural countryside grown up in dense hardwoods. Climbing soon on another ridge, you then come to a junction with Route 131 at 17½ miles. Go left here on Route 173 and 131, and head southwest along some fine stone walls into Searsmont. Rolling pasture yields to houses as you descend into the village and pass the Searsmont Town Offices and Library at about eighteen miles. Now cross a stream that drains Quantabacook Lake to the north. Going by the attractive Searsmont United Methodist Church and the village store, stay on Route 173 as it rises out of town, crosses the St. George River twice, and goes right at 18¼ miles, heading north. The St. George makes its way southward through a chain of lakes and ponds, reaching the ocean far southward between Cushing and St. George.

Travel west-northwest on Route 173 now, and then proceed westward in piney woodlands. Come to empty countryside where mixed-growth forest yields glimpses ahead to hills at 20¼ miles. Lots of hackmatacks line the road here briefly. Crossing another stream, you head more to the northwest and pass a Christmas tree farm and the Evergreen Valley greenhouses, going under a power line at twenty-two miles. Soon you drop to another settled area, pass the historic Georges River Grange, and cross the river once more at 22½ miles in South Montville. Climb westward out of town with beautiful views off to the left and south. There are excellent views in your rearview mirror, too. Up you go in open pasture and onto a ridge heading northwest, where there are more hill views in front of you.

Another passage through stone walls brings you into more wooded country and onto more up-and-down terrain. Views line up to the west of attractive Stevens Pond near an old farm. You pass a small dam and a boat launch as you cross the St. George River another time. Going northward you come to a stop sign, where you go left on Route 173 at a T, at 24½ miles. Curving and climbing north-westward steadily, you then come to the Liberty U.S. Post Office and some pleasant old homes and shops in the community of Liberty.

Liberty was once a bustling place. In the old days, two water-powered sawmills, a tannery, a gristmill, and a shingle maker provided employment. If you collect junk, there are a couple of places here that sell interesting and elegant junk, should you find them open. Moving on, you join Route 220 and, passing some more houses and the Walker School, go north to the junction with Route 3 at Clarks Corner, where this ride ends, at 26½ miles.

Route 3 can be followed west to Augusta, Maine's state capital, or east to your starting point in Belfast for other coastal destinations. A nice conclusion to a day outing in summer is to visit nearby Lake St. George State Park, just west of the junction of Routes 3 and 220. Camping is also available at this park.

Route 12

Augusta to Camden

Highway:
Route 105

Distance:
49½ miles (one way)

One of several routes offered in this book that link central Maine with the coast, Route 105 provides a pretty, rural meander from Augusta to Camden, from the state capital to one of Maine's most appealing mid-coast towns. In between, this trip takes you through several picturesque, tiny villages and then on to coast and mountains. Many thousands of people make this journey weekly, but they travel Route 17, a parallel but heavily used road that often has one coping with unwanted traffic.

The route described here is not only more scenic, it is usually about as free of traffic as a road can be. This route is pleasant to drive any time of year, but at its most attractive in foliage season, when you'll drive through miles of deciduous woodland lit up with those fiery colors that are so much a feature of Maine in September and October.

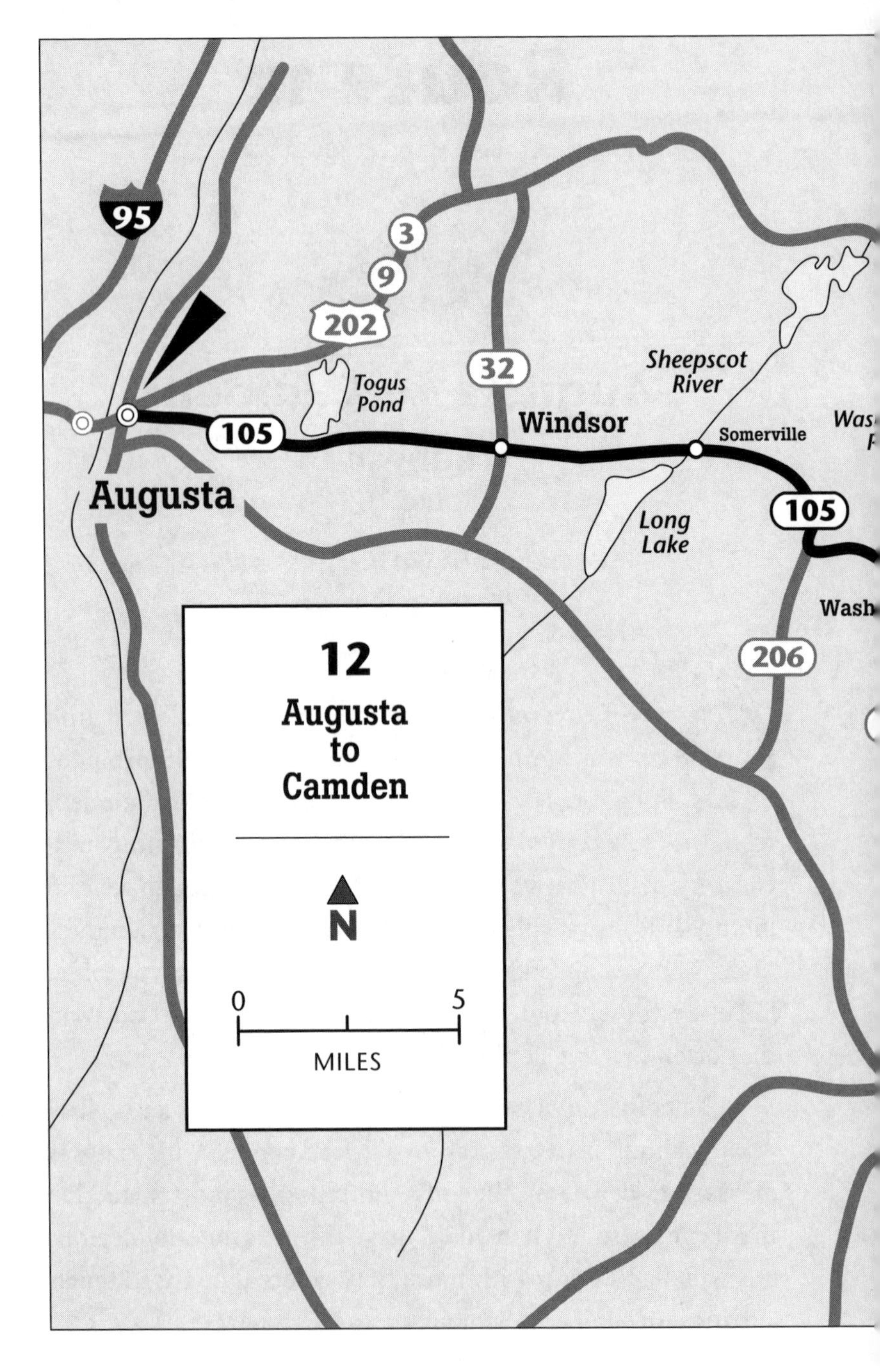
95
3
9
202
32
Togus Pond
Sheepscot River
Windsor
105
Somerville
Augusta
105
Long Lake
206
12
Augusta to Camden
N
0
5
MILES

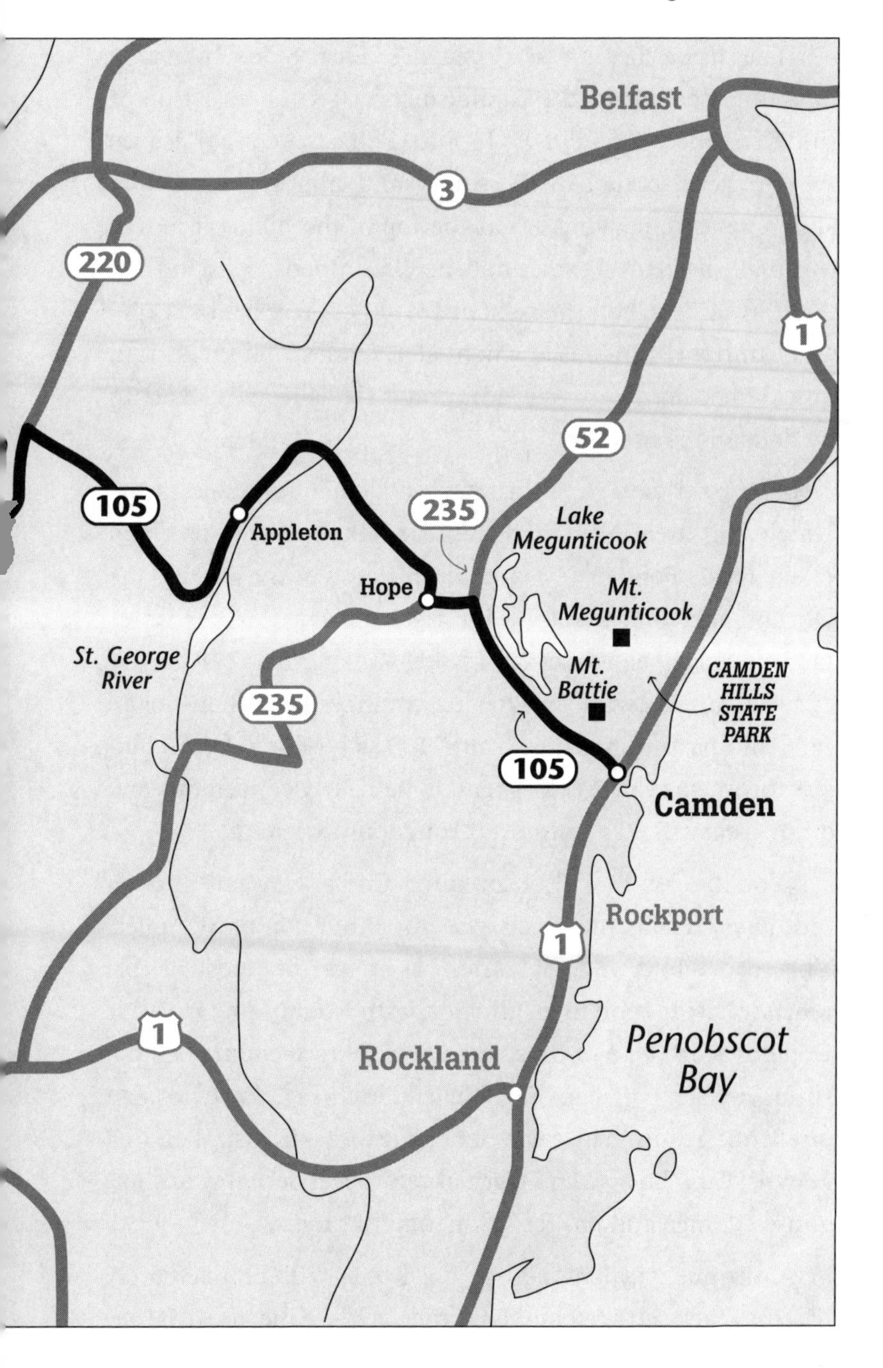
Belfast
3
220
1
52
105
Appleton
235
Lake
Megunticook
Hope
Mt.
Megunticook
St. George
River
Mt.
Battie
CAMDEN
HILLS
STATE
PARK
235
105
Camden
Rockport
1
1
Penobscot
Bay
Rockland

The drive begins at Augusta's East Side Rotary, a busy intersection in the capital district on the east side of the Kennebec. Route 105 (South Belfast Avenue) leaves the northeast corner of the rotary and climbs the hill by a shopping area, curving left at the top of the hill as it moves through pleasant residential neighborhoods, passing St. Andrews Church on the right at 1¼ miles. You'll cross Cony and Church Hill Roads at a light at 1½ miles, and the terrain quickly becomes more rural in pretty fields heavily overrun by dandelions in spring.

The road meanders through wooded countryside in the Hatch Hill area. You drive more northeastward soon and reach Togus Pond at 5¼ miles. Fine views of the pond to the left and a smaller marsh to the right appear. Further water views open up as you cross a bridge at six miles before you curve away eastward in wooded countryside. When not in field and pasture, most of Route 105 is bordered by deciduous forest, so foliage colors tend to be nearly continuous and quite spectacular in autumn throughout its length.

You'll cross the Windsor town line at 6¾ miles. High meadows, fields, and farms will surround you at 8½ miles. The road winds and dips often, as it will for most of this journey, rising soon to its junction with Route 32 by Husseys General Store, one of those increasingly rare country emporiums where you can buy almost anything. Its bold sign out front reads "Husseys General Store—Guns, Wedding Gowns, Cold Beer." An informal reference, perhaps, to shotgun weddings and the refreshments that follow.

Continue straight across on Route 105, immediately driving back into woodlands and fields. Guernseys graze in summer pastures as the road drops eastward. The route meanders through more open country, and drops to a stream and farmhouse at eleven miles, shortly crossing the intersection of Coopers Mills Road. Views are good here. The road winds eastward with occasional views to hills ahead in very rural country. Soon the road turns more northeastward, skirting the nearby (but hidden) Long Pond. At 14½ miles, you crest Turner Ridge in Somerville and, in minutes, cross the Sheepscot River.

More old farms and pasture-going-back-to-woods are passed as the drive runs up and down a series of rolling hills at 16½ miles, with the Somerville School and town offices appearing on your right. There are some daunting curves in this section; drive carefully. Climbing again, you are treated to some excellent views across farms and fields, and toward ranges of hills ahead to the northeast. You enter the Damariscotta Lake watershed at 18½ miles, and the views continue to expand. These pretty ridges feed nearby Damariscotta Lake with their runoff.

The road then descends to an intersection with Route 206, where you will bear left. Continue on Route 105 with more excellent views eastward over pasture and blueberry fields. The road skirts Washington Pond in Razorville on the left at 21½ miles, where there is a public boat launch facility with good views of the pond.

In minutes, you descend steeply to a junction with Route 220 in the little village of Washington. Established as Putnam in 1811, Washington is not much more than a bend in the road, with a general store (filling station), post office, bargain barn, and a couple of antique shops and gallery. Still, it has a nice flavor about it, and is reminiscent of many small Maine communities long vanished.

Route 105 now runs uphill and north out of town, passing the pretty Village Church, and climbing toward another rise. Many of the buildings of Medomak Camp lie along here. Soon you make a sharp right in South Liberty, turning east at 25¾ miles near the South Liberty Baptist Church. The winding, hilly route passes Muddy Pond on the right. You cross the Appleton town line at twenty-seven miles, and the road dips, fords a pretty brook, and loops more northward. You next continue through the neighborhood known as Burkettville, where you cross Collinstown Road, staying east. A dilapidated store and gas pump, long out of use, have collapsed and rusted into oblivion. Next you pass the Medomak Valley Grange, a reminder of the grange's important past in Maine farm country, on the right at twenty miles, near Pettengill Stream.

More winding, challenging driving awaits to the east as you continue toward Camden. Climbing Snow Hill, you drive southeast and east, crossing gravel Appleton Ridge Road at thirty-one miles. Here, you quickly level off in beautiful pasture bordered by a line of statuesque oaks that is especially attractive in autumn, and come to the junction with Route 131 at thirty-two miles. A large barn topped with lightning rods is to the left of the intersection. Pause here to enjoy spectacular views of Sennebec Pond backed by a range of striking hills to the southeast, directly ahead of you. You are high on Appleton Ridge with the kind of superb Maine views rarely seen by travelers wedded to the rush of congested turnpikes.

A left turn here on Route 131 and 105 takes you northward on a short descent to the village of Appleton, again not much more than a school and small store at an intersection. At the crossroads of this pleasant little town, founded in 1829, pause and take a right on Sennebec Road and drive to the bridge over the very lovely St. George River. Rumored to possess a trout or two, this stream makes its rambunctious way southward through the community winter and summer, as reliable as you please. Uphill, you pass the town picnic area, Appleton Town Hall and volunteer fire station, and a church. At the top of the hill at Gushee's Corner, make a U-turn around the flagpole and look back on the stretch of Appleton Ridge you have just navigated. When you're ready, descend again to the junction with Route 105 and turn right and northeast.

Head north, passing the Appleton Baptist Church on the left at 35¾ miles. Beautiful mountain views open up to the east in more farm country. The Camden Hills are sometimes visible. As you drive north, Route 105 (Searsmont Road) soon bears right and eastward again in North Appleton at a filling station. Here Route 105 is known as the Camden Road. Descending over the St. George River again, the road winds eastward, crests Blueberry Hill, and continues its up-and-down progress. Entering a settled area, you pass Bull Hill Road at forty-two miles, and pretty hillside pastures, dotted with cattle, emerge. At 42¾ miles, you reach the junction with Route 235 at the general store in Hope, another pleasant Maine crossroads. Continue east on Route 105 toward Camden, where views of Bald and Ragged Mountains soon appear rightward.

The route winds its way through stone walls, spruce, and hemlock as you come to the shores of Megunticook Lake on your left. There are a number of outlooks onto this majestic lake as you proceed. Cross Molyneaux Road and make your way into the west side of Camden village. Fine views of Ocean Lookout on ledgy Mount Megunticook and Mount Battie are on your left as you drive closer to town.

Your route drops into the town center and terminates by the converted mill buildings in the heart of Camden's shops and restaurants at 49½ miles.

Edna St. Vincent Millay's Camden is a very appealing Maine village, now discovered by well-to-do retirees from elsewhere, by summer visitors, and by yachtsmen plying Maine's coastal waters. Its near-perfect little harbor is host to a constant stream of sail and motorized craft in season, and a fleet of old schooners makes daily and weekly trips out of this port.

Many interesting shops, restaurants, bookstores, and galleries dot the center of the village and waterfront. Camden certainly deserves to be explored on foot, as an architectural legacy of lovely older homes has been widely preserved. A range of bed-and-breakfast establishments and inns will be found on U.S. Route 1 north and south of town, and on village side streets. Hiking in the nearby hills offers outlooks onto spectacular ocean and island scenery.

Route 13

Dresden Mills–North Newcastle–Jefferson–Waldoboro–Friendship

Highway:

Blinn Hill Road, Thayer Road, Routes 218, 194, 213, 32, 220

Distance:

42 miles (one way)

This interesting drive along a varied network of country roads from central Maine to the coast requires both hands on the wheel. No sleep-inducing four-lanes here. The route follows meandering back roads, some of them unnumbered, all the way from inland Dresden Mills, just below Maine's state capital, to tiny Friendship on the Atlantic. Despite being close to major population centers and even, on one occasion, crossing busy U.S. Route 1, the route described here wanders through farm, field, and woodland in highly pleasing rural countryside largely unmarred by "progress." One might say this route is, intentionally, the longest distance between two points, with hill views, farmsteads, and lake country in between, a delightful outing in all four seasons.

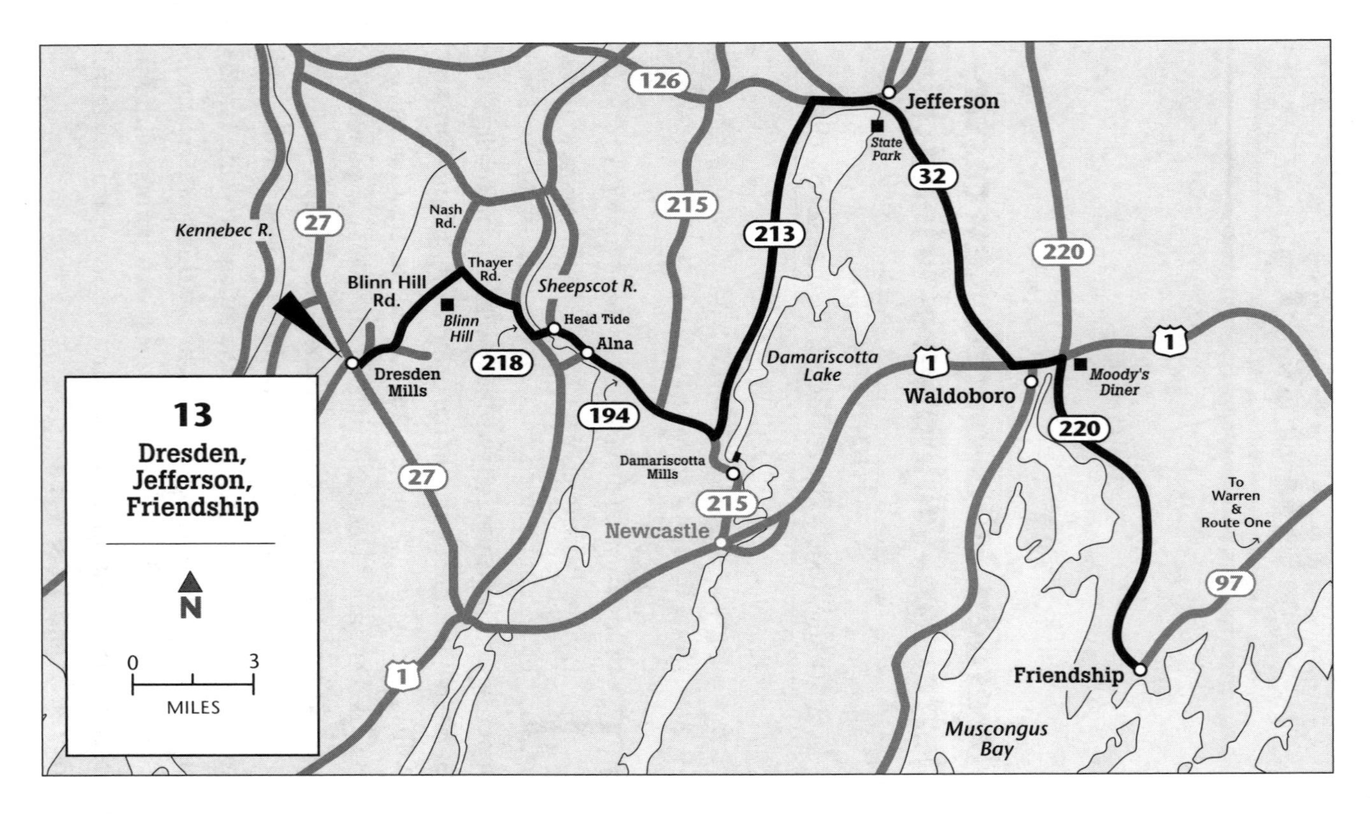
13
Dresden, Jefferson, Friendship
N
0
3
MILES
Kennebec R.
27
Blinn Hill Rd.
Dresden Mills
Nash Rd.
Thayer Rd.
Blinn Hill
218
Sheepscot R.
Head Tide
Alna
194
126
215
Damariscotta Mills
Newcastle
213
Damariscotta Lake
Jefferson
State Park
32
1
Waldoboro
220
Moody's Diner
To Warren & Route One
97
Friendship
Muscongus Bay

The drive takes off from the little town of Dresden Mills on Route 27, southeast of Augusta. Opposite St. Johns Episcopal Church follow Blinn Hill Road northeast out of the settled area. A sunken bog thick with dead trees borders the road to the right as you drive southeastward, soon entering pasture. Curving away from the town through fields with a ridge ahead, you pass East Pittston Road. You continue on Blinn Hill Road as it rises east and northeast at just over a mile, and you emerge in open blueberry fields and more pasture.

Small farms and scattered houses line the road as you climb slowly at two miles in deciduous woods. The grade increases, the woods drop away, and you emerge on open ridge with truly spectacular views from Blinn Hill to the distant horizon westward. These outstanding 180-degree views persist at 2½ miles while you continue along the ridge, pass the NOAA Weather Service radio tower, and proceed north. In clear weather, you will see into New Hampshire here, Maine's western mountains rising in the foreground against New Hampshire's Presidential and Carter-Mahoosuc Ranges sixty miles to the west. Some limited views to the right and east also occur on Blinn Hill, as do mountain views to the north as you begin to descend in more blueberry fields to the left.

Hill views continue ahead as you travel through pastures and woodlands, descending more rapidly, and, at 3½ miles, go over a little brook and climb northward. The road stays to the high ground on the hilltop, rolling pasture offering good outlooks to the east. Horses graze in fields as you arrive at a T at 4½ miles, where you bear right and southeast on Thayer

Road as the Nash Road goes left. Large blueberry fields, strewn with glacially deposited boulders, lie to the left as you continue in the direction of Head Tide through an area of few houses. Go through a slump and continue southeast onto another ridge with views rightward toward Blinn Hill. You'll pass sheep in pasture in pretty, rural countryside, and you soon go by an old barn on the left at six miles. The road rises to some treeless flat land covered with blueberries and joins the Wiscasset Road (Route 218) at 6¾ miles.

Go right on Route 218, dropping southeastward and crossing the Alna town line at 7¼ miles, near Anniversary Farm. (This route follows, for a short distance, a road described elsewhere in this volume.) You shortly come to a junction, where you go left off Route 218 and turn into Head Tide, approaching the dam on the left and crossing the bridge over the Sheepscot River.

Head Tide marks the limit of the Sheepscot's tidal waters. Go right and east on Route 194 and follow the river, which gradually pulls away to the right. Continue eastward over several rises and rejoin the river as it comes in on the right, well below a bluff. Staying with the banks of the Sheepscot, you proceed by the Alna Town Offices at a junction with Dock Road. The route strides east and passes Egypt Road at 9½ miles, crosses the Newcastle town line at just under ten miles, and reaches Route 215 on the left at 11½ miles. Here, Route 194 becomes Route 215 south, which twists and turns generally eastward.

You reach Route 213 at 13¼ miles, going left here on Bunker Hill Road, as Route 213 is known locally. Soon in open, rural country again, you pass small farms surrounded in pasture and proceed generally northward. Bogs lie below hill pasture dotted with attractive old farmhouses. The road rises and dramatic views of Damariscotta Lake open on your right. At 15¼ miles, you can get right down to the water's edge if you turn into the State of Maine boat ramp area on the right.

Beef cattle roam in fields along here, the road climbs again, and you pass Deer Meadow Farm at 15¾ miles. As you climb, you are traveling the length of Damariscotta Lake northward, and truly excellent views begin to appear at just over seventeen miles. A series of grand, dramatic outlooks appear far below to the east as you drive along the lake. Drifting up and down, the road rolls farther northward, with more water views to the lake and the hills beyond.

Watch for a marsh that feeds Deer Meadow Pond on the left at nearly eighteen miles. Open ridgeline pastures dominate here, and stone walls border the highway in deciduous woods in this little-settled country as more marvelous views of Damariscotta Lake appear at 19½ miles. The Camden Hills stand behind the lake, farther east. Dropping more northeastward, you go by old scattered farms and come to Route 126 (the Gardiner Road) on your left at 21¼ miles. Staying on Route 213, enter the settled area of Jefferson as the road curves eastward around the lake. Frequent water views appear by Damariscotta Lake Farm as you join Route 32 after 22¾ miles. Continue east on Route 32 through the village. Cross the inlet stream, go by filling stations and the town market, and follow Route 32 southeast as it passes the entrance to Damariscotta Lake State Park on the right at twenty-four miles. The park offers attractive lakeside picnicking and swimming in summer. A small admission fee is charged.

Run eastward on the Waldoboro Road (Route 32) past a commercial campground at 24½ miles, shortly passing the Maine Forest Service station. Drive through attractive, thinly settled countryside in mixed pasture and woodlands, and cross the Waldoboro town line at 26¼ miles. The road curves more to the southeast and south at Orffs Corner, continuing south with good views over rolling hills to the east. Roadside farms appear with cattle in the fields. You go by a fine marsh to the right at 28¾ miles, pass some other large working farms, and go over railroad tracks in Winslows Mills at thirty miles. Next you gradually descend as Route 32 winds through more rolling pastureland to the junction of Route 32 with U.S. Route 1 in Waldoboro at just under 40 miles.

At the lights, go left and north on U.S. Route 1 for a short distance and climb the hill. Just before Moody's Diner, bear right onto Route 220 and head southeast and south through Waldoboro center. (You may want to give in to temptation and have a big piece of fabled Moody's pie before going farther.) Waldoboro's pleasant main thoroughfare is lined with attractive older homes, the Waldo Theatre, churches, and services. Go left on Route 220, Friendship Road, at the lower end of Main Street and in the direction of Friendship. At 33¾ miles you will pass excellent water views to the right over the Medomak River. Climbing southeast in rural country again, there are further broad, high outlooks to the striking Medomak as it broadens to a bay.

Marshy fields and woodlands border the route to your left as you pass Blue Sky Farm at 36¾ miles. Route 220 stays with the high ground at the top of this rib of land as it runs through pretty South Waldoboro at thirty-eight miles, where there are bed-and-breakfast establishments. After forty miles, most houses disappear and the country is forested as the road winds considerably. You cross the Goose River at the Friendship town line, having driven 40⅓ miles. You enter a somewhat more settled area as the road winds up and down the ridge. Go down through a gully and climb again at 42¼ miles. You rise shortly to the center of Friendship, coming to a T with the town library dead ahead. Go right and conclude this drive at Archie Wallace's Store (filling station, groceries) opposite Shipyard Avenue.

Side streets lead down to the waterfront. Fine views of Hatchet Cove and Friendship Harbor are eminently worth taking in. There are also ocean views from nearby Martin Point (you passed the connector road a few minutes ago, coming into town). Ask locally for directions. Inn accommodations are available opposite the library.

From Friendship, you may return northward by retracing your route, or you can head east and north to U.S. Route 1 via Cushing and Warren on Route 97, also an attractive drive.

Route 14

Thomaston–Port Clyde–Owls Head–Rockland

Highway:
Routes 131, 73

Distance:
42 miles (around loop)

The St. George River is separated from the open ocean for a considerable distance by a peninsula that dips southward from Thomaston and culminates, some fourteen miles farther south, in the pleasant seaward village of Port Clyde. The peninsula, composed mainly of the townships of South Thomaston, Owls Head, and St. George, is one of those many fingers of land that jut out from Maine headlands and create unique little neighborhoods quite unto themselves. It forms an uneven neck that falls southward into the Atlantic, bordered to its east by a dozen little islands that seem to have migrated from its midriff. The area has long been attractive to artists, both visual and literary: Sarah Orne Jewett's acclaimed *Country of the Pointed Firs* was written in St. George.

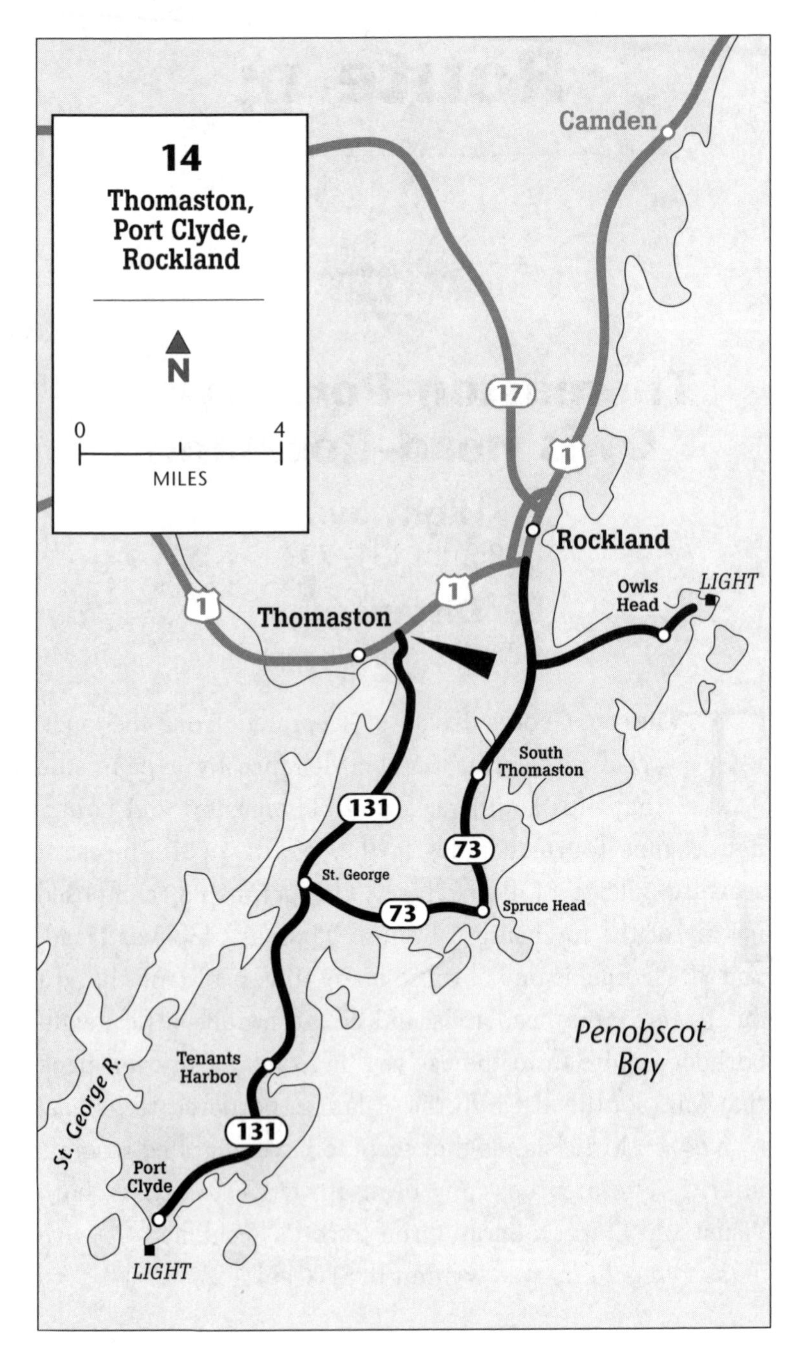
14
Thomaston, Port Clyde, Rockland
N
0
4
MILES
Camden
17
1
Rockland
Owls Head
LIGHT
1
1
Thomaston
South Thomaston
131
73
St. George
73
Spruce Head
Penobscot Bay
St. George R.
Tenants Harbor
131
Port Clyde
LIGHT

This journey wends its way down the peninsula all the way to Port Clyde and then comes back up, veers eastward, and takes in Owls Head, with its famous lighthouse, before fully regaining the mainland at Rockland. If you enjoy hugging the coast, you'll discover a certain contentment along these easy country roads that march to the sea.

You leave U.S. Route 1 at the north end of Thomaston, itself a pretty midcoast town replete with old houses of character on a hillside that glides easily down to a small, protected harbor. From U.S. Route 1 take Route 131 by Montpelier, the lordly, reconstructed manor house of General Henry Knox, a great proprietor who, with other principals in the Waldo Patent, controlled much of the land in this area after the American War of Independence. Knox was a shrewd and persistent bargainer whose wealth increased steadily until changing political fortunes and betrayal by those who had done his dirtiest bidding drove him to penury. Montpelier stands as a monument to his and his wife, Lucy's, penchant for ostentation.

Drive southeast on Route 131, with Thomaston Harbor off to the southwest. The little Finnish Congregational Church stands by the road. Finns, Russians, Swedes, Norwegians, and other ethnic groups earlier lodged in small coastal settlements along the Maine coast. Family names still suggest their presence here and there. The outstanding Maine photojournalist Kosti Ruohomaa, offspring of the Finnish coastal clans, found his way into the larger world with a camera. Past Riverview Farm (1767), fields soon open down to the coves. This is Andrew Wyeth country, and well down the opposite peninsula stands the famous Olson House, which Wyeth's art immortalized. Field roses line the roadside as you drive by scattered farms, following a high rib of land.

The road soon leads into St. George, where you pass the junction with Route 73. Climbing Route 131 southeastward at 7½ miles, you have occasional pretty views west to Watts and Cutler Coves. At 8½ miles there are leftward views to Long Cove, backed by Clark Island. Just over nine miles below Thomaston, you enter Tenants Harbor, with its cluster of attractive old houses and working waterfront off to the left on a short loop road. Route 131 makes a sharp left at the Tenants Harbor Baptist Church, with more water views following. At 11½ miles you drive through the little hamlet of Martinsville. A sign reflects the brevity of your visit with typical Maine restraint. It reads: "Welcome to Martinsville. Come again."

Ocean views become more frequent now, and scattered islands lie beyond Mosquito Harbor. At 14¼ miles, a side road to the left leads to Marshall Point Museum. Just beyond, you enter Port Clyde, pass the post office and inn, and descend to the waterfront. Port Clyde boasts a vigorous working shoreline with a local fishermen's cooperative, and passenger boats departing for Monhegan Island daily. The general store and a few other shops offer supplies and refreshments. The broad harbor is best seen from the two main piers that lie behind the general store. Parking for those taking the *Elizabeth Ann* or *Laura B.* to Monhegan is here, too. A leisurely stroll around the village, following quiet roads leading off in various directions, will handsomely repay your curiosity.

Back at the wheel, drive north away from the waterfront and take the right turn leading uphill to the Marshall

Port Clyde's Marshall Point Light

Point Museum. Follow a narrow road east and south to Marshall Point Light, where you'll find excellent outlooks to the open Atlantic and barrier islands. The lighthouse is currently operated as a museum by the St. George Historical Society and is open to visitors from May through October. The light was established in 1832 and the present tower erected in 1857. The keeper's house, now headquarters of the museum, was built in 1895. An interesting tour of the museum will acquaint you with the history of the area, and a small contribution will help keep important preservation work ongoing.

Next, head back to Route 131, turn right, and drive north. Watch for the junction with Route 73 noted earlier. Bear right on Route 73 and travel northeastward in sparsely settled country. (Set your odometer to zero again at this junction.) At 2⅓ miles along Route 73 you cross the South Thomaston town line in an area dotted with coves and fields. Climb a hill and descend into Spruce Head, where the road makes a sharp left, turning north. At 4½ miles you're back in wooded countryside, passing next through marshy ground. At 6¾ miles you drop to the water again, shortly crossing the Weskeag River. The pleasant river views merit a brief stop and perhaps a walk around. You pass the Weskeag Historical Society Library and the South Thomaston Post Office in a few more moments as you continue north on Route 73 at 7¾ miles.

Owls Head Light

The Owls Head Transportation Museum, with its airfield, lies to the right at 8¾ miles, while views to the Camden Hills are ahead in the distance. Just beyond here, turn right for Owls Head Light, driving eastward by the Owls Head Grange at just over nine miles. Views to Rockland Harbor appear on the left. After climbing a birch-covered hill at ten miles, you continue eastward, where you make a left by the Owls Head General Store and Post Office at 11½ miles. Follow this rural street and shortly bear left once more onto Lighthouse Road at just under twelve miles, soon passing a beautiful harbor to the right. Watch for lighthouse park signs now, and reach lighthouse parking at $12^1/_3$ miles. Seasonal comfort facilities and picnicking are available here. A short walk brings you to the much-photographed lighthouse and splendid views from the promontory.

Next, retrace your $3^1/_2$-mile drive from the lighthouse back to Route 73, and bear right. Head north now to Rockland, with good harbor outlooks along the way. In minutes, you reach the built-up area of Rockland and soon emerge in the downtown shopping area at a junction with U.S. Route 1 at eighteen miles (on Route 73). The visitor will find Rockland is home to many interesting stores, waterfront accommodations, and eating places, and worth exploration.

Route 15

Castine to Deer Isle

Highway:

Routes 166, 199, 175, 176, 15, and local roads

Distance:

44 miles (one way)

Castine ranks as one of Maine's most lovely towns. A truculent frontier area in the days of our Colonial forebears, it lives on today a quiet, manicured place, rife with fine old homes and pretty tree-lined streets. Castine is the kind of town to which you come to shoot a period film when you hope to capture a fine sense of unspoiled time and place. At the mouths of the Bagaduce and Penobscot Rivers, Castine has long been a seafaring town, and, not surprisingly, the campus of Maine Maritime Academy is here. There are no towns close by to the north, so Castine carries on a well-satisfied separateness, off by itself at the end of a peninsula, discretely hidden from open ocean by Islesboro and Cape Rosier.

Castine happens also to be one of those places kicked about during the early days of the Republic and before. It

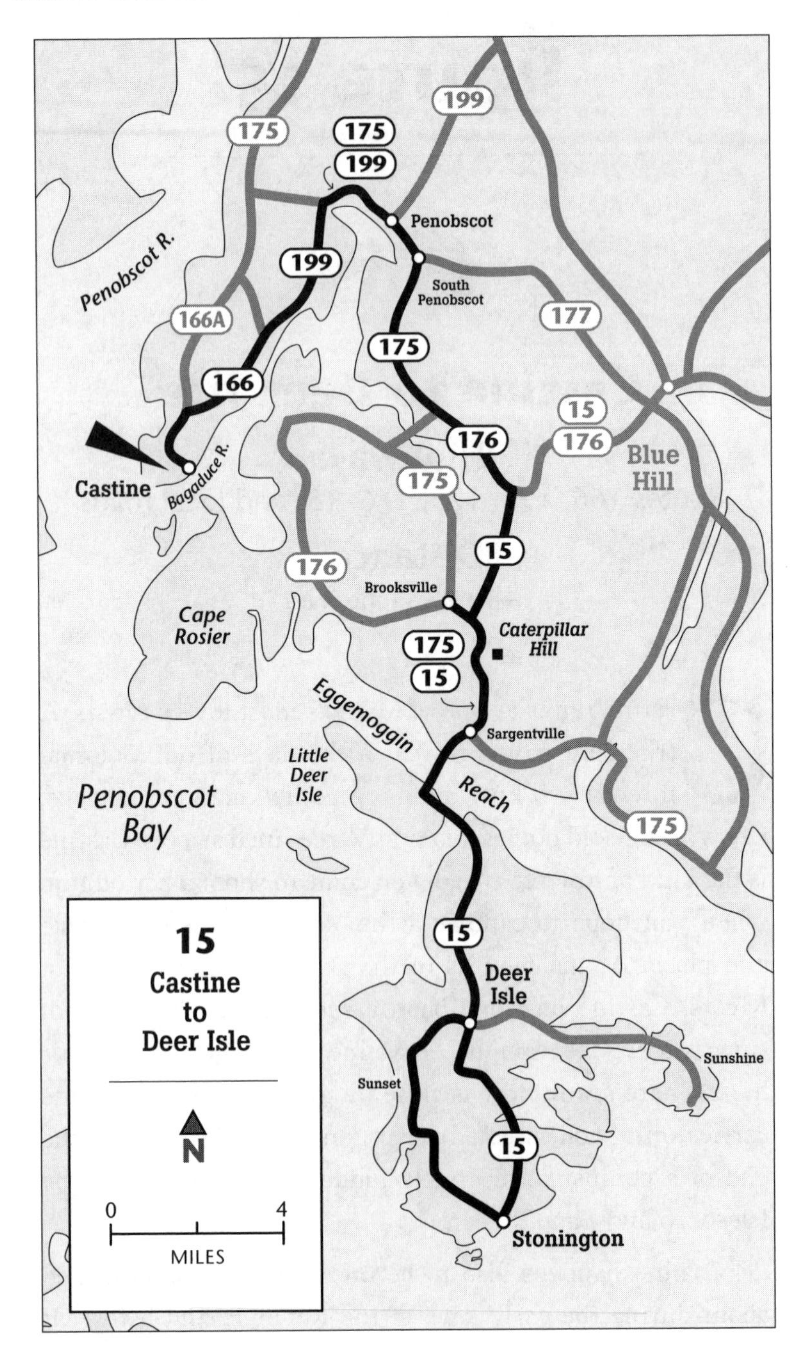

175
175
199
199
Penobscot
Penobscot R.
199
South
Penobscot
177
166A
175
166
15
176
176
Blue
Hill
Castine
Bagaduce R.
175
15
176
Brooksville
Cape
Rosier
Caterpillar
Hill
175
15
Eggemoggin
Sargentville
Little
Deer
Isle
Reach
Penobscot
Bay
175
15
15
Castine
to
Deer Isle
Deer
Isle
Sunshine
Sunset
N
15
0
4
MILES
Stonington

Down the hill to the Bagaduce: Castine village

passed first through the hands of the French, who established a trading post named Pentagöet here around 1614. The British took it away. The Dutch held it for a while. The upstart American rebels got their hands on it, only to lose it to the British again in one of the most humiliating naval defeats of the Revolutionary War. The Nova Scotia–supplied British constructed Fort George on the outskirts of town in 1779 in an attempt to hold on to these northern reaches of Massachusetts even as the Revolution wound down. The British came back and occupied Castine again during the War of 1812, but left for good in 1815. Now, of course, we own it again.

After a brisk stroll around town admiring the local architecture, we'll begin our drive here by the remains of the old fort's embankments on Battle Street, opposite the academy's Desmukes Hall.

You drive out of town on Route 166, passing the golf course, and, heading north, soon go over a canal that cuts across the neck. This tidal ditch, once big enough for longboats carrying armed troops, was dug by the British in 1799, and provided quick waterborne transport of men from Hatch Cove on the east to Wadsworth Cove on the west. You come to the junction with 166A, keeping right on 166 at 1⅓ miles. Next drive up through pretty, rolling countryside, reaching the Penobscot Cemetery on the right in three miles. At just under four miles, bear right on Route 199 and follow it toward Penobscot as it tracks along the orchards, coastal pastures, and coves of the upper Bagaduce.

After cresting Perkins Hill, Routes 199 and 175 come together at 7½ miles, and you bear right at their junction, heading east and southeast on Route 199 and 175 through Penobscot and South Penobscot. At nine miles, the road drops to the waterside, with splendid outlooks southward onto Northern Bay. Stay with Route 175 after it separates from Route 199, continuing southeast in the direction of Sargentville. Watch for a small picnic area by the water at 9½ miles.

You proceed southward through unsettled rural country at 10⅓ miles, shortly passing Route 177 and Bagaduce Hall. Pine, hackmatack, spruce, and oak woods close in again. You stay left with the main road as it becomes Route 176 at just over fourteen miles by a general store. (Follow signs to Sargentville, Deer Isle, and Stonington.)

The road now runs along the northeast side of the Bagaduce Falls to a junction, where 176 goes left to Blue Hill and you continue south now on Route 15 (Snows Cove Road). Blueberry barrens, knee-deep in stones and boulders, dot the roadside as you climb southward in very rural ground. The Sedgwick Elementary School is on the right at 18⅓ miles.

Route 15 rejoins Route 175 at 19½ miles, and following Route 15 (Caterpillar Hill Road), you enter Brooksville, continuing southward. Pause at the state rest area on Caterpillar Hill, where there are 180-degree, spectacular water views over Eggemoggin Reach toward the faraway Camden Hills. Your route ahead to Deer Isle also is visible. Reaching a T at 22½ miles, bear right and stay with Route 15 at Sargentville, driving west and south to Byard Point, where you cross to Little Deer Isle on a wonderful, steep suspension bridge. An information center, open seasonally, lies just on the other side.

The route, at 25½ miles, next runs along a narrow causeway with fine views back toward Stave Island and Eggemoggin Reach, which you have just crossed. Carney Island lies immediately offshore to the right. You climb southward again on Route 15 toward the community of Deer Isle, going by the Island Nursing Home and Care Center just beyond twenty-seven miles. The modernistic Deer Isle–Stonington High School is on the left. Passing several bed-and-breakfast establishments, you descend into the village of Deer Isle at just over 30 miles. Anyone who enjoys the visual arts will want to pause in Deer Isle and make a tour of the various photographic, craft, and art galleries in

The waterfront at Stonington

the small square. In summer, a number of talented artists, craftspersons, and photographers display here.

Heading south again on Route 15, you climb the hill out of town past the Congregational Church, Deer Isle Elementary School, and Town Hall. At 30¾ miles you drive by a road to the nationally famous Haystack School of Crafts and the village of Sunshine, worth a side trip if you have time. Good cove views to the left and right appear here, too. The road crosses another channel and enters Stonington proper at 35¾ miles.

Stonington has an interesting main street, with striking harbor views, shops, and restaurants. The community is perched on a hillside facing the sea, mansarded old houses rising in tiers up the hill. Largely undiscovered until recent years, Stonington is now fighting the battle to remain itself while real estate values rise with in-migration, and less affluent, native families find it tempting to sell up and move on. This is an old story on the Maine coast, of course. Many towns once wedded to fishing and lobstering have become second-home or retirement communities for the well-to-do from away. In the process, the very character of those towns has changed forever. For now, Stonington holds on.

When you've explored the village, follow the main street above the working waterfront and head westward out of town, passing a pretty inlet on the left at 38¼ miles. You pass the road to Burnt Cove and continue by boat shops and repair facilities. On your left, about two miles out of the village, watch for Whitman Road. Up this side street is the Nature Conservancy's Crockett Cove Woods, a tract of beautiful, densely wooded land with walking trails donated by artist and architect Emily Muir. (See the author's *Walking the New England Coast* [Down East Books] for a full description.)

This northward, meandering road enters Deer Isle again at just under forty miles. Going inland near Crockett Cove in wooded country, you pass the Deer Isle–Stonington Historical Society at 41½ miles. Fine hillside views leftward across the bay toward Camden appear again shortly before you reach the Sunset Post Office at forty-two miles. The road drops to the northeast, and good views open west to the water and also inland here. After crossing a causeway as you continue northward, at nearly forty-four miles, you enter Deer Isle village again, this time from the southwest, and conclude this drive.

Travelers will find an enjoyable introduction to this region in the days before the turn of the century in Mary Ellen Chase's classic *A Goodly Heritage*. Chase appealingly reveals the experiences of her childhood in the region around Blue Hill in years of great simplicity in rural, coastal Maine.

Route 16

Bingham to Jackman

Highway:
U.S. Route 201

Distance:
50 miles (one way)

Far to the northwestern corner of Maine lies what has been called "moose alley." US Route 201 follows the Kennebec River to its confluence with the Dead River and then continues onward, all the way to Canada. This drive, which stops just short of the international boundary, follows U.S. Route 201 into the isolated, wild country of the upper Kennebec. And this is moose country par excellence. Roadside signs warn of moose crossings and urge wary driving. These large animals are denizens of a supremely attractive, largely unsettled region of mountains, streams, lakes, and dense woodlands eminently worth visiting. On this northern journey, you'll stay close to the banks of the Kennebec, prime rafting country, and pass through several fabled, tiny villages that are more outposts than developed communities.

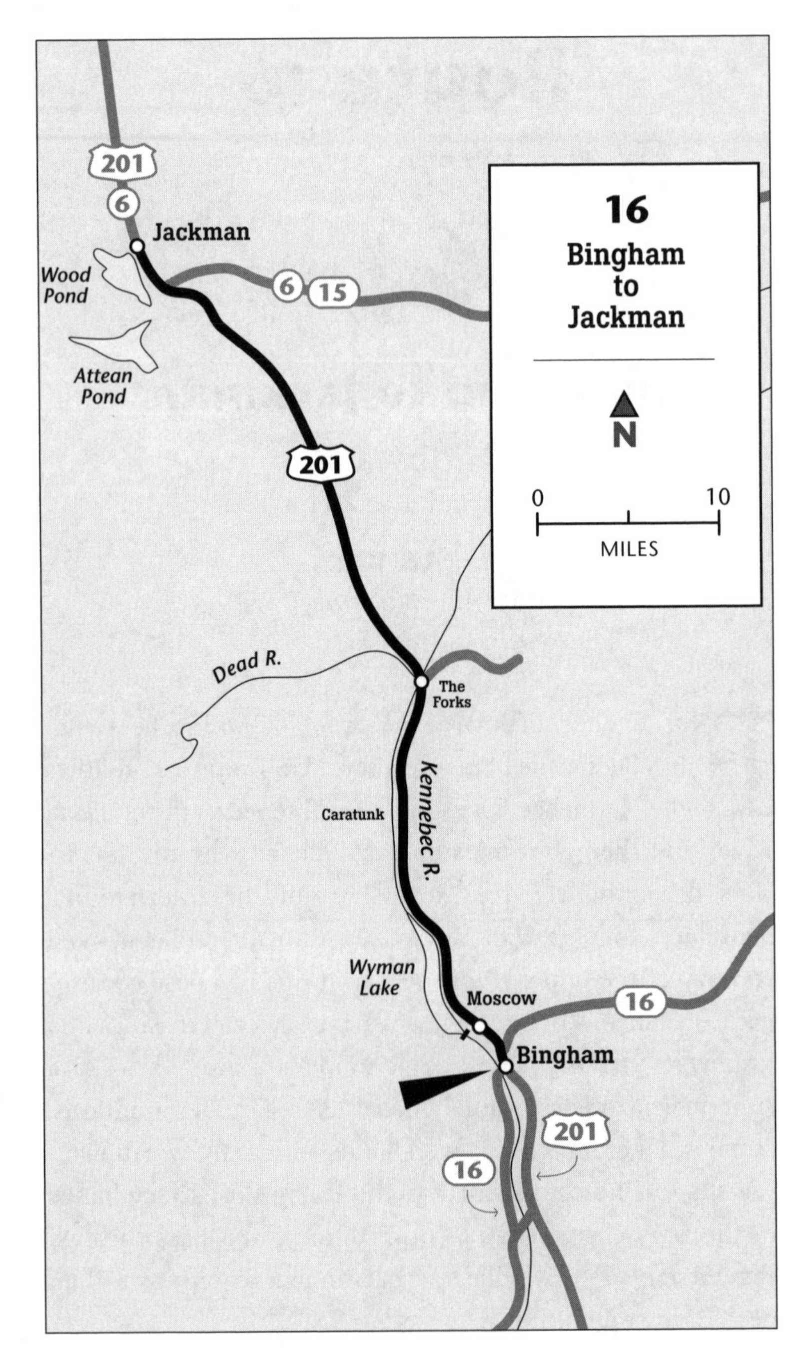
16
Bingham
to
Jackman
N
0
10
MILES
201
6
Jackman
Wood Pond
6
15
Attean Pond
201
Dead R.
The Forks
Kennebec R.
Caratunk
Wyman Lake
Moscow
16
Bingham
201
16

South over Wyman Lake in the Kennebec

Your journey begins at the junction of Route 16 with U.S. Route 201 at the north end of the business district in the small river town of Bingham. Leaving town, you cross Austin Stream on U.S. Route 201 and head northwest through Moscow. Passing schools, you are soon in open country, rolling through a series of bends, where you pass a ski area and climb a hill westward. Spectacular views of the Kennebec occur immediately, and, at 2½ miles, you come to the dam that backs up the Kennebec to form Wyman Lake. Pleasant Ridge stands above the west side of the lake. U.S. Route 201 stays with the shore of this lake, and then the Kennebec, as it alternately climbs higher and then descends to the shore again at just under four miles. The road pulls away from the lake occasionally, only to return again, offering more fine views upstream. Numerous turnouts provide off-road lakeside parking.

After several miles of lakeshore travel, you head northwest at 6½ miles. At nine miles, watch on the left for a state rest area where Wyman Lake narrows at its north end.

Pause here for excellent views southward down the lake from a high bluff. The Kennebec resumes its channel now, and you will follow it northward as the road goes around Cates Hill in Caratunk. Climb another ridge at eleven miles for more dramatic views of the river. You'll see several islands here, and you'll pass the Caratunk boat launch at just under fourteen miles. An inn and the first of numerous rafting operators are located along this stretch of road, and moose warning signs begin to appear as you cross Pleasant Pond Stream. Continuing northward, you go by the Maine Forest Service office at 15¾ miles and take in still more Kennebec River shoreline.

This is the river country favored by the legendary Dud Dean, Maine Guide, a rural character created by Maine writer Arthur MacDougall Jr., whose three classic collections of Dud Dean stories—*Where Flows the Kennebec, Under a Willow Tree*, and *Dud Dean and His Country*—are a staple of any serious fisherman's library and a delight to read. MacDougall wrote of the river in its prime, when oversize browns and fine salmon were plentiful.

The now frequent moose warning signs are a necessary regional reminder to watch carefully for the lumbering presence of *Alces alces americana*, the eastern moose, which, as noted earlier, frequently makes appearances at northwoods roadsides or casually ambles in front of cars. The number of these giant herbivores increases yearly, and with it the frequency of auto-moose encounters seems to grow also, a rising toll of bent sheet metal and moosehide. There were roughly ninety-five unplanned engagements between moose and automobiles on this road in a typical, recent year.

The view northwest: Moose River Bow Trip country near Jackman

After crossing Holly Brook, you go by Martin Pond and the Pooler Ponds on the right and left, entering the Forks Plantation at just under seventeen miles. Several of these impounded ponds just above the level of the river are visible along here. Running to the northwest, U.S. Route 201 drifts away from the river for a moment as you come upon more rafting outfitters.

Proceeding northward, you head away from the small settlement and drive straight north in heavily wooded terrain, next crossing Kelly Brook at 20⅓ miles, with more water views leftward. The Kennebec runs in two channels momentarily. Go by The Forks Town Hall at twenty-two miles, and soon arrive at a junction with a side road to Lake Moxie and Indian Pond.

The Forks are so named for the convergence of two great rivers here. The Kennebec curves northeastward from our route and runs to man-made Indian Pond, and thence to its origins in Moosehead Lake. The inaccurately named Dead River comes to this junction with the Kennebec from the west, arising miles upstream in the Chain of Ponds and Coburn Gore. It was up the Kennebec and thence westward on the Dead that Benedict Arnold and his troops traveled in 1775 on their way to oust the British from Quebec. The Arnold expedition still stands as one of the great military miscalculations of all time. Arnold's men lugged bateaux (shallow, flat-bottomed boats) and gear up through merciless streambeds and icy swamps, and over wintry mountains in search of the route to the Quebec plains. Floundering about in appalling conditions, Arnold's half-naked, near-starved men perished in the cold, turned back, or disappeared into the dark woods. Those that did eventually reach Quebec were foiled in their pathetic attempts to rout the enemy. Interestingly, Arnold's ill-fated attempt on Quebec was approved and encouraged by a fellow named George Washington.

At 23½ miles, in West Forks, you come to a state rest area and are soon in a built-up region, with bed-and-breakfast establishments, commercial campgrounds, outfitters, and a general store (last gasoline). The road goes up Moulton Hill at twenty-five miles and moves along a plateau with more moose warning signs to remind you of the animals' presence. Good views eastward occur at twenty-seven miles as the road runs northwest. You climb along the side of Johnson Mountain and then back north again in a straight stretch in wild, wooded country. After a run through boggy land with views forward, you come shortly to the southwest shore of beautiful Parlin Pond at almost thirty-seven miles, where you'll find a state rest area.

Resuming travel northward, you cross the Parlin Pond town line at 37⅓ miles, run through a small settled area, and are soon in attractive wooded countryside again with more pond views rightward. Climbing again at forty-one miles, the road heads northward, crests the rise, and enters Jackman. Some truly excellent mountain views west and north open up now.

At 43⅔ miles, you encounter another hill and arrive at a scenic overlook above and right. Here there are exceptional views westward over one of those spellbinding lake and mountain panoramas that are often characteristic of northwestern Maine. On clear days, one can see into Canada.

The road descends gradually toward the center of Jackman, with more mountain views ahead at forty-six miles. The road then works northwest, and broad views from northwest to east open up as the village becomes visible ahead. Descending into a settled area while running more westward, you arrive at the built-up town of Jackman and go by the entrance to Attean Lake Camps at 48¾ miles. You pass a local historical society museum at forty-nine miles, and, on the right, you soon pass the old Canadian-American Railroad station. Wood Pond is the large body of water to the left as you drive down Jackman's main street. This trip ends now, at the Jackman Tourist Information center at 50¼ miles.

Lodging, stores, outfitters, and restaurants are located here. A variety of accommodations can be reserved for short stays or full vacations. Staff at the tourist information center are helpful. A quiet place, Jackman nonetheless offers fishing, boating, hiking, camping, hunting, snowmobiling, and other outdoor sports. The town is the starting point for one of Maine canoeists' favorite river journeys: the Moose River

Bow Trip. Jackman is also the last major settlement before going north through Moose River, Dennistown, and Sandy Bay Township, then crossing into isolated, rural Quebec.

Route 17

Jackman–Rockwood–Greenville

Highway:
U.S. Route 201, Route 6

Distance:
48 miles (one way)

This drive offers a west-to-east cruise across the mountain and lake country of Maine's northwest kingdom, a route that spans the woodsy distance between three isolated towns in an area of great beauty. Candidly, the route begins and ends north of north. So, we have here an excursion for those already well upcountry who want to navigate from the state's border with Canada to Greenville, in the heart of the Moosehead Lake region.

This journey begins in the northwest border town of Jackman, a rangy, old-fashioned community where fishing, camping, boating, and hunting are major pastimes and night-clubs or glitzy shopping centers are in short supply. What Jackman lacks in worldliness it makes up for in hospitality and grand scenery. The town lies at the heart of a network

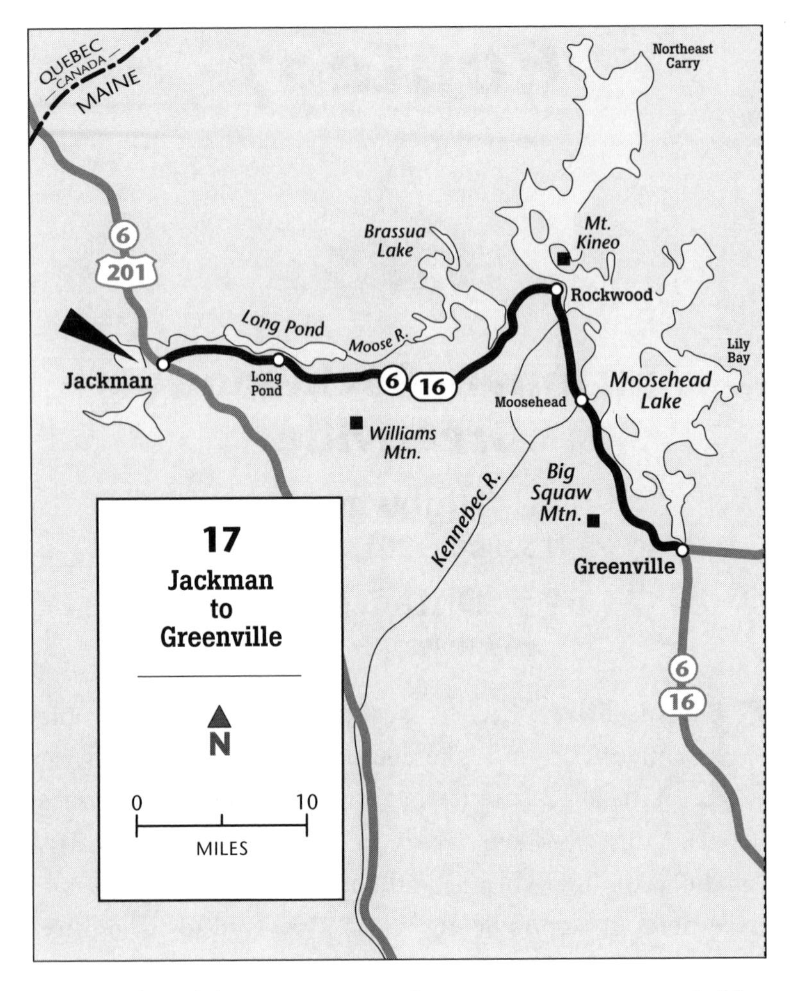

of legendary lakes, streams, and canoe routes surrounded by places with names like Misery Township, Moose River, and Upper Enchanted Township. Local landmarks like Number 5 Mountain, Little Gulf Stream, Burnt Jacket Mountain, and Sugar Berth Pond abound. This is an area for people who love the outdoors and a better place to vacation than a lot of the more crowded and expensive resorts farther south. It's a good locale, too, to begin a backcountry drive.

Parlin Pond, south of Jackman

From the center of Jackman you drive south a short distance on U.S. Route 201 to its junction with Route 6. Here you turn left on Route 6 and commence the northeastward journey toward Long Pond and Rockwood. You soon move away from the settled area, and there are nice views in your rearview mirror back toward Burnt Jacket and Sally Mountains on the far side of Attean and Wood Ponds. Good outlooks north and east to the surrounding country appear as you move into a wooded area and cross Halfway Brook in the land of fast-moving, heavily loaded logging trucks. The road follows a high plateau with lake views back left through the trees and, here and there, glimpses of the Moose River to the north.

The driver is forewarned that he or she is in the midst of moose and deer country here. It's interesting to watch for animals, but a certain vigilance is required. Moose are fond of stepping into the road just in front of you, and then staring as if with injured dignity. Watch your speed at all times.

At 5¾ miles, water views appear on the left and immediately you enter Long Pond Township. You come to the Upper Narrows of Long Pond, and then follow the south shore of this extensive body of water for a couple of miles. The tracks of the Canadian-American Railroad also cling to Long Pond's shore. You draw away from the waterline at the Lower Narrows and run southeast, crossing Parlin Stream in boggy country at ten miles. Climbing another hill, you reach an area where a lot of clear-cutting has been done. These cuts tend to be screened from the road by a thin band of standing trees—a "beauty zone"—but one can see the devastation nonetheless.

You enter the Sandwich Academy Grant at just over thirteen miles, running parallel to the unseen Moose River, which connects Long Pond and Brassua Lake to the north. Mountain views occur through occasional open spots in the dense cover. The route follows the side of Misery Ridge as it works eastward. Go through some rock cuts at just over fifteen miles as views of major mountains appear ahead to the northeast. Having passed the hidden Otter Ponds, the road leans around to the northeast and crosses and then follows North Branch Stream in an alder swamp. Drive next through some fine stands of old-growth white pine and reach still more slightly regenerated clear-cuts.

At 21¼ miles you cross the Canadian-American Railroad tracks in the tiny settlement of Tarratine and catch glimpses of the southerly tip of pretty Brassua Lake to your left. Traveling almost at water level, you follow Brassua for nearly two miles, round a bend by the lake, and continue northeast. You climb a grade soon, staying with the Moose

River as it connects Brassua Lake with Moosehead Lake in what is known as the Rockwood Strip at twenty-three miles. Roughly twelve miles wide and thirty miles long at its extremities, Moosehead is New England's largest lake. The road works its way around to the south as grand views of Moosehead appear and you enter Rockwood at 28¾ miles.

Most striking here is the dramatic outline of 1,800-foot, rock-faced Mount Kineo, a key area landmark and an inspiration to writers from Henry David Thoreau onward. Thoreau first came to the Moosehead region in 1846. His frontier experiences on that and subsequent trips are recorded in *The Maine Woods*, published in 1864. No finer introduction exists to what this region was like more than a century and a half ago. Thoreau climbed the Precipice Trail up Mount Kineo in July 1857. The great expanse of lake before him he called "a suitably wild-looking sheet of water sprinkled with small, low islands which were covered with shaggy spruce and other wild wood."

You now drive south, headed for Greenville as the road crosses the West Outlet of the Kennebec River. Mountain views lie ahead as you motor south, and there are views through the trees to Moosehead as you pass a commercial campground on the lake at 30¾ miles. Cross the rail line again and go over a bridge that spans the East Outlet of the Kennebec River in Moosehead at thirty-six miles, where, in season, you are likely to see trout and salmon fishermen working the waters. You soon go by Deep Cove on the left. Impressive mountain views lie before you: the outline of multipeaked Big Moose Mountain to the southwest in Big Moose Township. Moving through fields, the road heads southeastward in sparsely settled countryside. Some cutover areas, dense with slash, line the road here, too, at 42½ miles.

At forty-four miles, turning more eastward on Route 6, you enter Little Moose Township and descend into a more settled area of motels, hotels, and camps as you get closer to Moosehead Lake once again.

Going south still, you drift into Greenville Junction, where the Canadian-American Railroad now runs above the road on a trestle. Stay on Route 6 and follow it past a seaplane base and through a built-up area of shops, accommodations, and services as it runs into Greenville. You reach an intersection with Greenville's main street at 48¼ miles.

Greenville, like Jackman, is one of the northwoods' most important outposts. It is the gateway to the Moosehead region and, via Kokadjo, to the network of timber roads that lead to the Roach Ponds and, well beyond, to Katahdin. For more than two centuries it has been the site of a number of great hostelries for visitors, lumbermen, and others passing through. Outfitters, guides, shops, tackle dealers, inns, and restaurants are all located here today. At the top of the hill, south of town, the chamber of commerce is a center for useful information on attractions and accommodations in the area.

Route 18

Howland to Vanceboro

Highway:

Route 6

Distance:

75½ miles (one way)

This drive covers the eastern half of the "Trans-Maine Trail," Maine Route 6. It will take you from Interstate 95 in Howland, north of Bangor, eastward to the Canadian border at Vanceboro and St. Croix. The route makes its way through attractive, rural countryside in a section of Maine not much traveled, particularly by visitors. From about its midpoint on eastward, the part of Route 6 described here lies in mostly undeveloped country—wild, forested, and remote. At the end of this journey the traveler will find the Canadian border at the tiny hamlet of Vanceboro on the bank of the St. Croix River. The route also provides those travelers who cross the boundary with access to the St. John River Valley in southwestern New Brunswick via St. Croix and McAdam.

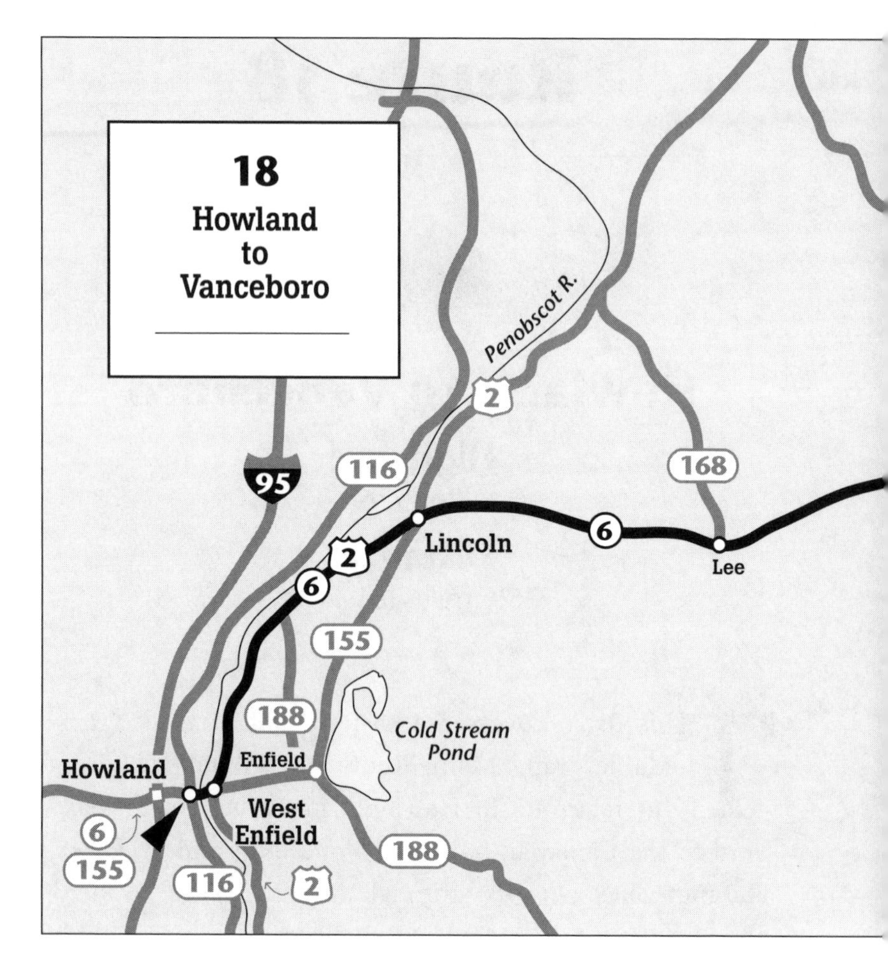

Begin at the junction of Routes 116, 6, and, 155 in Howland, just east of the Howland exit on I-95. Following signs to U.S. Route 2, you travel eastward on Route 6 for a short distance, and then cross the broad Penobscot River at a junction where the Piscataquis River joins the main channel. Having crossed the Penobscot, you are in West Enfield, where you pass the post office and, in one mile, go left and north on Route 6 and U.S. Route 2. Quickly you roll through

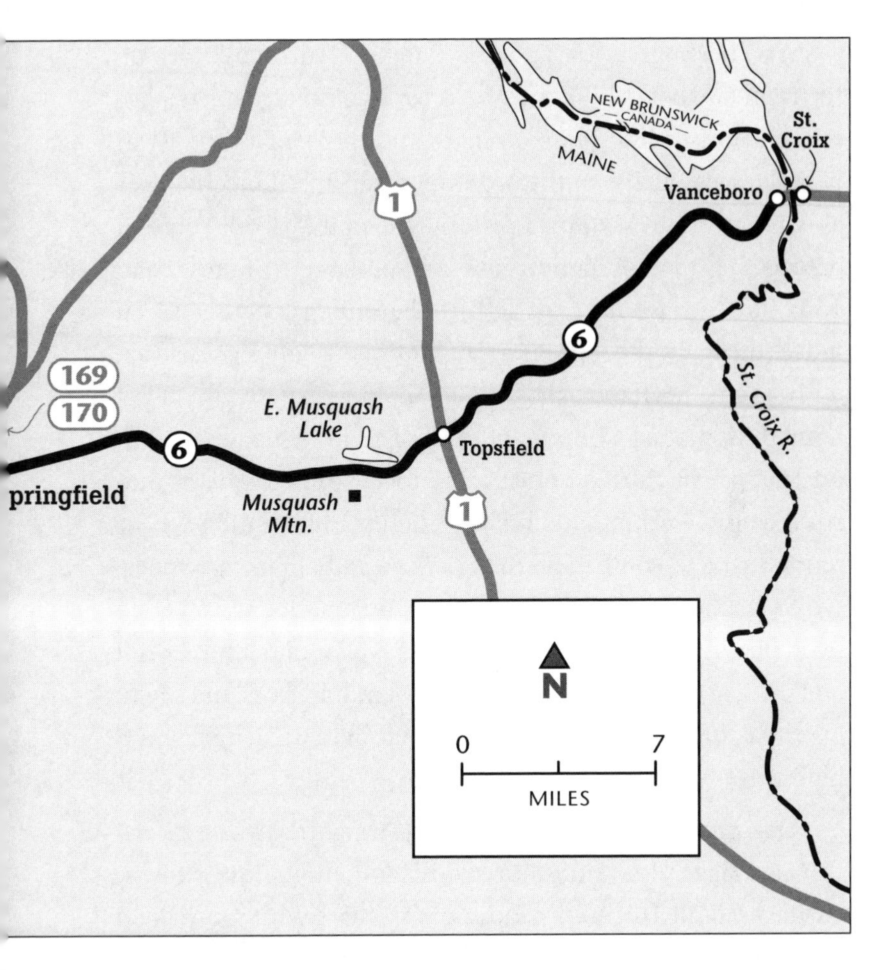

a business district, and then enter open country with scattered houses, passing Green Valley Golf Center at 5½ miles. Continue to the east of the Penobscot in wooded country grown up in hackmatacks and hardwoods. Leave Enfield for Lincoln at 7¾ miles on a tableland, passing a state rest area on the right at nearly eight miles. Public boating access to the Penobscot is available on the left at 9⅓ miles, below Mohawk Rapids.

At 11¼ miles, you pass the Bangor Hydro buildings on the right and come into Lincoln. A series of unattractive malls and businesses line the road here, and the odor of the Kraft paper process wafts southward from the nearby Lincoln Paper and Tissue mill. Ask anybody locally, and they'll tell you that odor is the smell of money, jobs, prosperity. At Routes 6 and 155, and U.S. Route 2, go left by the military statue as you move through the appealing downtown shopping district, with pretty Mattanawcook Pond to the east. By the First United Methodist Church and a Civil War statue, keep right on Route 6 at thirteen miles. The road heads eastward into rural country again and climbs as pretty, rolling hills appear to the east and south. The road rises steadily in dense woods, while making a series of winding, up-and-down traverses over ribs. At just under twenty miles, you climb another hill and come to low boglands with dead standing trees and, then, open pasture. You cross the Lee town line at 21 miles on a high ridge with good southerly views.

Descend through a series of long straightaways eastward to Lee village at twenty-four miles. You climb out of town, passing Route 168, and continue northeast with more good outlooks from high pastureland, entering Springfield at twenty-eight miles. Crossing Wright's Stream, the road offers fine views ahead to the northeast and north as you crest more hills at 29½ miles. Pass Springfield Congregational Church at 32½ miles and soon go through a junction with Route 169 and Route 170.

You are soon in Carroll Plantation at 34½ miles, and climb a series of hills where you can see the straightened road far ahead of you. Your rearview mirror shows the long, ruler-straight road you have just traversed. More striking views appear ahead at thirty-seven miles. Mountains to the east and south become visible. The low mass of Bowers and Getchell Mountains lies just to the south. The route crosses Lindsey Brook shortly, where pasture borders the road, and then heads southeastward as you go by the Baskahegan Stream deadwaters to the left. The area is part of a series of connected streams and dri-ki-filled marshes that are attached to isolated Baskahegan Lake to the north. Edmund Ware Smith immortalized this remote country in his interesting and often humorous outdoor stories in *To Hunt and Fish in Maine.* At 41¼ miles you cross into Kossuth Township and enter Washington County.

On the south shore of East Musquash Lake

You now pass more cutover lands that are growing back, bisected by a series of logging roads. Excellent views appear ahead to low mountains. You are in the heart of productive timber country at 44½ miles. Pass the entrance to Maine Wilderness Camps on hidden Pleasant Lake at 45½ miles. Route 6 runs through some S-curves and continues on the flat, then climbs another rib with lake views to the northeast. Running due east again, the route crosses Alder Brook and approaches East Musquash Lake, reaching the Topsfield town line at forty-eight miles. The road widens and descends at 49½ miles, with increasingly fine views of the lake, backed by Farrow Mountain. A state rest area with picnic tables on the left overlooks the shore of unspoiled East Musquash Lake. Musquash Mountain rises across the road to the south, and fine, broad panoramas appear up the lake toward Brooks and Walden Brook and Stuart Brook.

Leaving this very attractive site, you continue east past Farrow Lake and Lathrop Heath, passing through a corridor of birches to a junction with U.S. Route 1 in Topsfield at 53¾ miles. Go straight across U.S. Route 1 and continue east on Route 6. You'll see signs for Vanceboro and Canada here. Route 6 narrows and climbs past an elementary school and enters Codyville at 55⅓ miles. The road winds to the north, slabs Hunt and Kane Ridges, and dips and rolls eastward with good outlooks to hills ahead and to the northeast. A roller-coaster ride carries you unpredictably eastward in dense, second-growth forest. Logging staging areas appear from time to time, and human habitation is conspicuous by its complete absence. Traffic on this road, with the exception of the occasional overloaded and flying logging truck, is nearly nonexistent. Leaving Codyville at Crooked Brook Stream, the road enters Lambert Lake Township at 63½ miles on a high rib of land.

Going through more dri-ki bog at 65½ miles, you enter a built-up area and cross the Canadian-American Railroad tracks, going east again. You reach the Vanceboro town line at just over sixty-nine miles, and the road pulls sharply to the southeast, goes through some S-curves with fine views to the northeast and, at 70¾ miles, recrosses the railroad line. The climax forest and low, boggy growth here—grown

Salmon fishing on the rapid St. Croix

up in pine, hackmatack, mixed hardwoods, and spruce—is typical of Maine's deep woods. You drive over another rise and come to a settled area, passing the U.S. Post Office in Vanceboro at 74¾ miles—the old railroad depot lies to the left (the author's father was once station agent here in long-gone, busier days)—and proceed around to the left on Route 6, arriving shortly at the U.S. Customs Station at 75½ miles, where this route ends.

You may complete your journey here, returning west toward Topsfield and U.S. Route 1, or cross the river to the Canadian side. New Brunswick Route 4 will take you eastward to the towns of St. Croix and McAdam. It is worth stopping here for a while by the banks of the lovely St. Croix River, which flows southeastward to Calais, forming the border between the two countries all of its length. The river has its origins in the nearby Chiputneticook Lakes to the northwest. In season, fishermen ply the falls below the dam in search of salmon. Canoe trips often depart here for the long run down the St. Croix to the sea.

Route 19

Island Falls to Lincoln

Highway:
U.S. Route 2

Distance:
53 miles (one way)

Parallel to Interstate 95 but on the other side of Molunkus Stream and, later, the Penobscot River, US Route 2 rolls south from Island Falls in deep woods, over high ridges with spectacular views of Katahdin and Baxter State Park, on south to Macwahoc and Mattawamkeag, and thence along the Penobscot into Lincoln. With the exception of the area right around Lincoln, it is possible to drive this route rarely seeing another car from Island Falls southward. The drive begins in Aroostook County amidst high potato fields and ends in Penobscot County in the shadow of great pulp yards and paper mills.

The center of Island Falls lies just east of Interstate 95. Begin on U.S. Route 2 at a bridge that crosses the combined

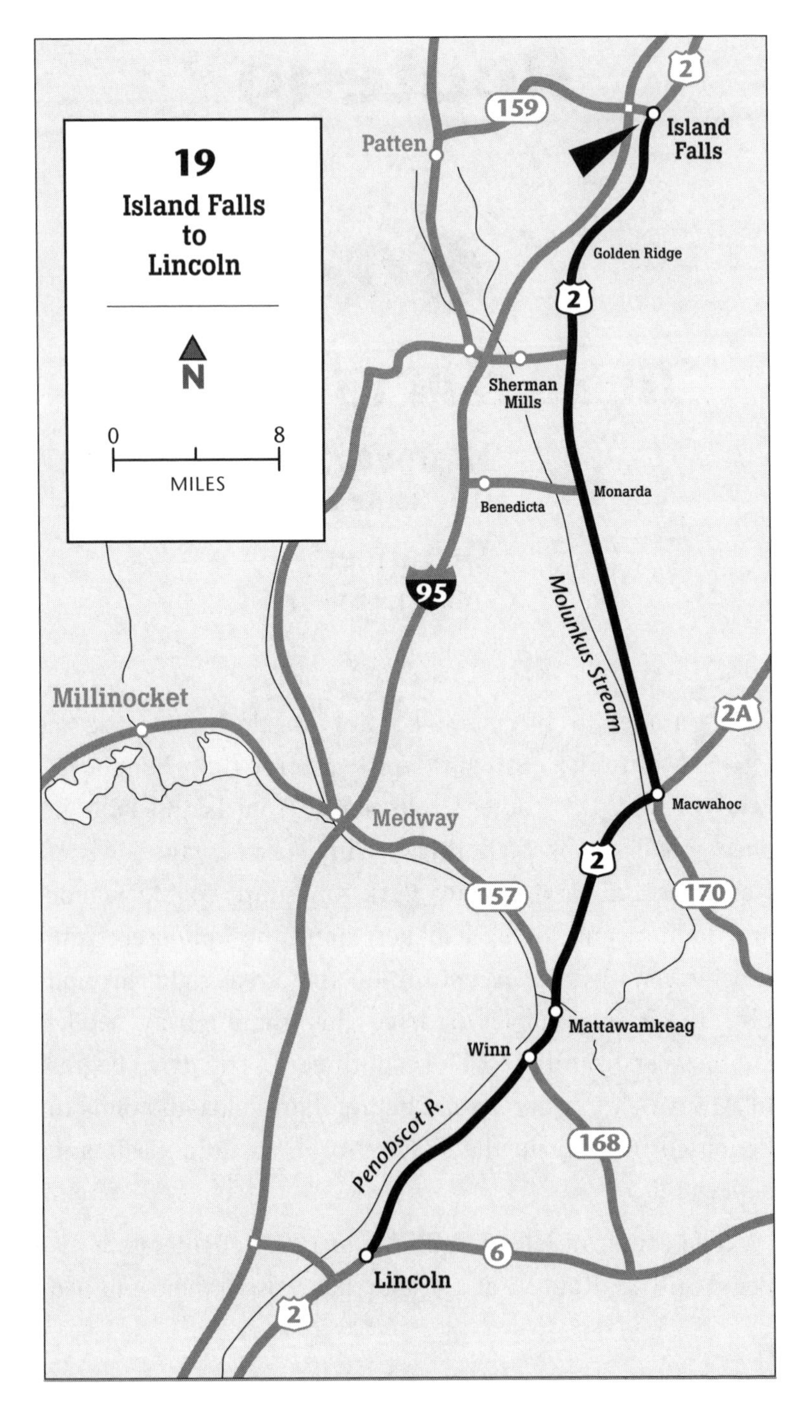
19
Island Falls
to
Lincoln
N
0
8
MILES
159
2
Patten
Island
Falls
Golden Ridge
2
Sherman
Mills
Monarda
Benedicta
95
Molunkus Stream
Millinocket
2A
Macwahoc
Medway
2
157
170
Mattawamkeag
Winn
Penobscot R.
168
6
Lincoln
2

waters of the Mattawamkeag River, Fish Stream, and Sly Brook in Island Falls. All of these watercourses come together a mile or so upstream. There are attractive falls below this bridge where the river heads eastward around an island for a short distance to Upper Mattawamkeag Lake. In spring, the torrents here are highly impressive.

Go south out of town on U.S. Route 2 toward Lincoln, by some pretty old houses and barns, cross Sly Brook, and head into open country at just a mile. You emerge in farm country and climb steadily into dense hardwoods and occasional hilltop fields where potatoes are grown. Farmhouses backed by potato fields lie on both sides of the road as you continue. Mountains appear to the southwest, and ahead are the high mountains of Baxter State Park, topped by the great, flattened mass of Katahdin, Maine's highest peak. On a clear day, these may be the finest views one can find of the mountains in Baxter State Park and to the north.

Henry David Thoreau, America's great prophet of simpler living and the natural world, came to Katahdin in September 1846. In his journal he wrote: "The tops of mountains are among the unfinished parts of the globe, whither it is a slight insult to the gods to climb and pry into their secrets, and try their effects on our humanity." Thoreau did not quite reach Katahdin's main summit, and turned back after an exhausting bushwhack through dense woodlands off the accepted path east of the Abol slides.

The road dips southward in a series of curves, enters Crystal, keeping right on U.S. Route 2 at 4¼ miles. Northern harriers circle in the sky on the next ridge as horizon-to-horizon views continue of Katahdin and mountains to its south. You go by more potato fields and farms at 5¾ miles. Keep left at a junction and go farther in high, rolling pastures with potato houses at eight miles in the Golden Ridge section of Sherman.

Gravel roads lead leftward to hidden Macwahoc Lake as you approach Woodbridge Corner and the junction with Route 158. The road clings to the high rib of land in open fields with broad panoramas in all directions at 10¼ miles. Going by Route 158, you continue straight ahead toward Lincoln, with mountain views to the left amidst more farms. Cross into Silver Ridge at twelve and 12¾ miles as you run straight south toward Monarda in mixed-growth woods.

Good views are ahead at fifteen miles, with further views off to the southwest now, too. Old barns and farms in front of pastures line the road as you crest another hill at seventeen miles.

Going more southeasterly, the road crosses Spaulding Brook and offers more fine outlooks to mountains in the west over rough fields of goldenrod. You reach a state rest area on the left at 20½ miles by Gulliver Brook, and you briefly leave T1R5 to cut through the corner of Upper Molunkus Township. In moments you cross Henderson Brook in the North Yarmouth Academy Grant.

The route winds southeasterly next in pretty, mixed-growth countryside with good views ahead from a plateau to rolling ridges off to the west, and you shortly cross Lower Henderson Brook. There are no houses here at all for miles. At 25¾ miles you come to Macwahoc Plantation and descend gradually, reaching another state rest area on

The Mattawamkeag River at Island Falls

the right on the banks of attractive Molunkus Stream. A stop here is in order. This rest area is perched right above the stream and offers pretty outlooks to the northwest and downriver. Further stream views appear through the trees to the right as you drive on. Keep right and south at a junction with U.S. Route 2A in Macwahoc (store). Then keep right and west again on U.S. Route 2 at a junction with Route 170, where you cross Molunkus Stream in a boggy area.

U.S. Route 2 continues west in low ground and curves gradually around to the southwest and south in unspoiled country again as you enter the town of Molunkus at 31½ miles and pass Aroostook Road. Going through a flooded marsh, you continue straight south at 33½ miles as you come nearer Mattawamkeag. You reach the junction of U.S. Route

2 and Route 157 and cross the Mattawamkeag River in the town center, going over railroad tracks where the Maine Central and Canadian-American Railroad meet. Just south of Mattawamkeag you begin to get glimpses rightward of the Penobscot River around Five Island Rapids. The road hugs the east bank of the river, and the railway line stays with the road, to the left, for miles.

You soon cross Houston Brook, drive through Winn at 40½ miles, and then go by Brown Islands Rapids in the Penobscot. Passing Snow Island and Sebonibus Rapids, too, you are shortly in more open country as you cross the Maine Central tracks at 42¼ miles. More Penobscot River views appear at a turnout and boat launch at 43¼ miles. Entering a more built-up area, you cross the Lincoln town line at just over forty-six miles. Lincoln bills itself as "The Town of Thirteen Lakes," but it is equally well known as a center for the pulp and paper industry.

The Penobscot is still visible by some old farmhouses with big barns, and then you encounter more residential sections at 49¾ miles. You cross the railroad line once again as you enter the center of Lincoln at 50½ miles. River views to the right appear behind houses and fields occasionally as you drive beyond a lumber mill and school. Lincoln's industrial centerpiece, the giant form of Lincoln Pulp and Paper, appears away to the west as you get closer to town and reach Lincoln's Town Hall and business center at just under fifty-three miles.

Route 20

Topsfield to Houlton

Highway:
U.S. Route 1

Distance:
55 miles (one way)

Topsfield is a mere crossroads where Route 6 and U.S. Route 1 exchange glances and then go their separate ways. It nestles in the heart of timber country, in the sparsely inhabited woodlands of Washington County, well north of Calais, south of Danforth, and minutes west of the Canadian border (see also Chapter 18—Howland to Vanceboro, Route 6). U.S. Route 1 north of Topsfield traverses the marshy deadwaters north of Baskahegan Lake and Crooked Brook, roams through quiet countryside with spectacular water views of the Chiputneticook Lakes, clings to high hillsides, and rolls on into potato country as it nears Houlton. Should anyone ask, this is the real Maine.

A little reassurance: Here U.S. Route 1 is not the frustrating, traffic-clogged artery it manages to be in summer many miles away in southern and midcoast Maine. Instead, most traffic, if there can be said to be any, bypasses this sec-

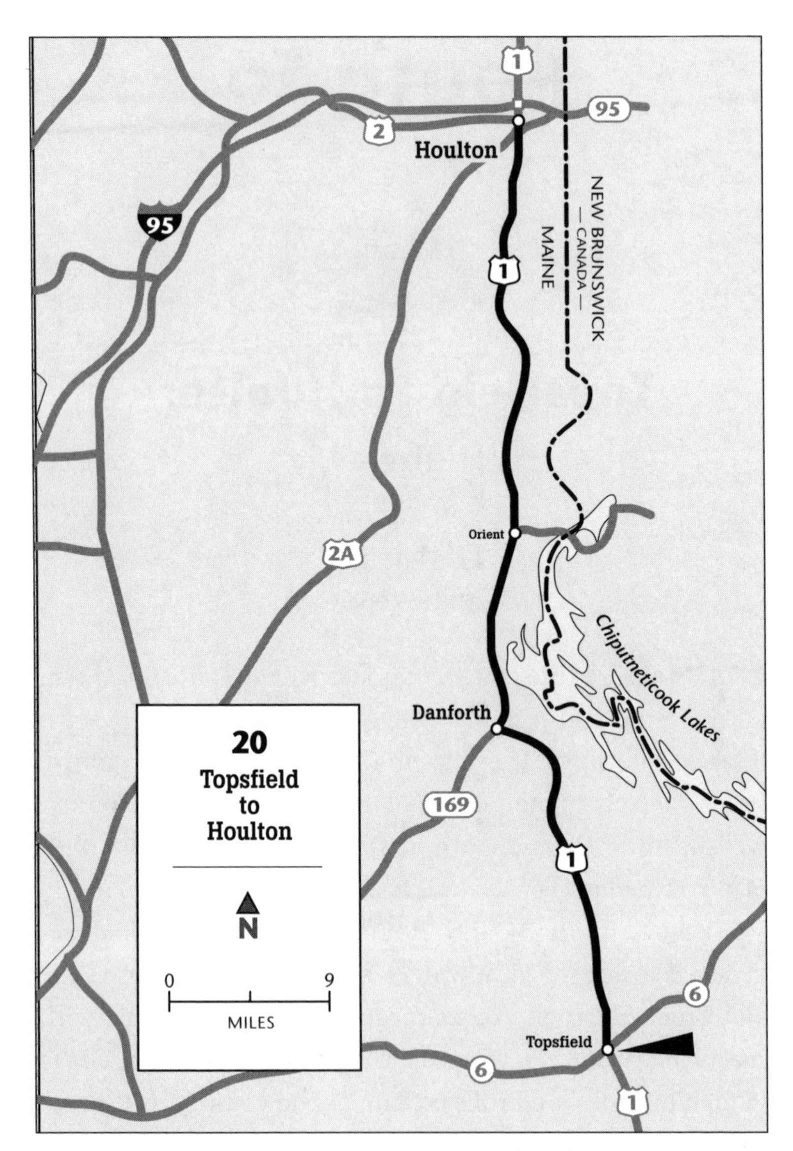

tion of U.S. Route 1 by traveling I-95, leaving this a lightly traversed country road of considerable charm and one of the few sections of this 1,800-mile route from Fort Kent, Maine, to Key West, Florida, still pleasant to drive.

Beginning in Topsfield, then, at US Route 1's junction with Route 6, roll toward Danforth. You drop northward out of Topsfield and, running in a straight line, go through some high pastureland and then by dense hardwood stands. This is pretty, rolling countryside with fields dropping off to the right. Climbing, you pass Tracy Mountain and make a long descent in more woods with mountain views ahead. Go by Little Tomah Lake and crest a hill with good northward views through the trees, and then drop to boggy ground grown up in swamp maples. Clusters of ferns and maples, white pines, spruces, and other mixed growth border the road. Woodlands here have been selectively cut. You cross into Brookton at just under seven miles and get up on a ridge with limited views to the left and to the right toward Vanceboro.

Go through a settled area and by a general store, the Brookton Baptist Church, the Brookton Community Center, and the Brookton Pentecostal Church at a crossroads at 8½ miles. The road to the right runs in to Jackson Brook Lake and Drake Lake. The road to the west leads to the northern shores of Baskahegan Lake. Keep north on U.S. Route 1 in more woodlands and swamp maple–dotted bogs. Good views leftward to mountains appear at 11½ miles as the road rises, and you proceed west and drive over the Danforth town line at 13¼ miles.

Go over the rail line in Eaton and cross two brooks that flow down from the Crooked Brook Flowage. At 18¼ miles you pass a public boat ramp and private camps as the road curves northwest. Pleasing hill views lie ahead and westward. Pass a school shortly and enter Danforth village, then stay right and north on U.S. Route 1 at its junction with Route 169 at 20½ miles. There are little settlements farther north, but Danforth (gasoline, stores, services) is the only town of any size on U.S. Route 1 from here to Houlton.

Danforth is the gateway to the beautiful Chiputneticook Lakes, expansive waters that straddle the border with Canada. From Danforth drive north, crossing into Aroostook County at nearly twenty-two miles. Now in Weston, you move through a spruce plantation and then fields, climbing to superb views as you run northwesterly. On clear days you can see perhaps forty miles to the north and west from this point. Once off the ridge, you pass side roads to camps and outfitters and, at twenty-five miles, begin to enjoy spectacular perspectives eastward over Grand Lake, the largest of the Chiputneticook chain. Peekaboo Mountain is ahead to the left. The views eastward continue as you move north, and you are soon over Brackett Lake, Longfellow Lake, and, farther off now, Grand Lake, passing the town offices of Weston at twenty-six miles.

Fine lake views continue as you move through more elevated, rolling countryside at 28½ miles. Pass a commercial campground, crest another hill, and slab alongside a wooded ridge with occasional views into New Brunswick. At 31½ miles you pass a side road in Orient that runs around the north end of Grand Lake and then on to Fosterville, New Brunswick. U.S. Route 1 now runs north through boggy territory on both sides of the road, and a state rest area is on the right at 35¼ miles as you approach the Amity town line. You traverse rather flat country now, and then rise in broad pastureland with excellent views east and southeast above treetops. Next you pass several farms on a high plateau, with ridge views ahead at thirty-eight miles.

The outlook eastward to Canada, Chiputneticook Lakes region

Though farmed and sparsely settled, this remains wild country. The author and accompanying photographer saw a full-grown puma (mountain lion) cross the road here at midday on a recent autumn drive. Maine Department of Inland Fisheries and Wildlife personnel report other puma sightings in this area, possibly of animals that have crossed from even less populated country over the border in New Brunswick. A controversy rages as to whether pumas are reestablishing themselves in Maine in small numbers, or people like me are seeing things. No mistake, we indeed saw a rare, big cat here, something neither of us expected to witness in our lifetime.

At 40½ miles, you drive through more high meadows and begin to enter potato country. Beautiful views to the right appear again as you pass a wildlife conservation center at 41¼ miles. Descending off the high ridge, you come to Cary at 42½ miles. The road runs north and crosses some brooks that connect with the larger Meduxnekeag River to the immediate west, where fine leftward panoramas stretch for miles.

At 48⅓ miles, you enter Hodgdon Corners and go through a developed area. U.S. Route 1 skirts the east edge of the town of Hodgdon. The author glimpsed a man skinning a bear in his dooryard on his last trip by here. You soon pass farms with silos and potato fields on another high ridge at 50½ miles. Cattle roam in fields to either side of the road. Then follows a familiar scene in Aroostook—potato processing plants, potato harvesting equipment, and fields being harvested (in autumn).

You next go over the Houlton town line, with the town center visible ahead. In an attractive residential neighborhood you drive by bed-and-breakfast establishments and the First Baptist Church and emerge in the heart of downtown Houlton by the courthouse at fifty-five miles.

Houlton is the shire town of Aroostook County and a major hub of commercial and agricultural activity at the southern end of the great Maine potato belt that runs north toward Presque Isle, Van Buren, and Madawaska. Maine is one of the nation's leading potato growers, and people here, if they aren't involved in lumbering, are likely to farm potatoes. Kids are let out of school in the autumn to help with the potato harvest and earn a little money. Houlton has a downtown shopping district adjacent to the courthouse and post office, and outlying malls offer additional supplies. Interstate 95 crosses into New Brunswick, Canada, on the northern outskirts of Houlton. U.S. Route 1 continues north to the northernmost tip of Maine at Madawaska and then dips west to its terminus at Fort Kent. Travelers who wish to return south from Houlton by a different route can use I-95 to Bangor, Waterville, Augusta, and Portland.

Route 21

Smyrna Mills to Ashland

Highway:
Routes 2, 212, 11

Distance:
42 miles (one way)

Well up into Aroostook and west of its major population centers, Route 11 follows the edge of the great woods, a north-south artery roaming the back of beyond. This drive covers a section of Route 11 and connecting Route 212 that finds its way through dense woodlands, potato fields, mountain ridges, and lumberyards in Maine's northernmost county. The route clings to high places and provides exceptional views of the wild mountain country in western Aroostook and Penobscot Counties, including Baxter State Park in Piscataquis County.

This route begins on U.S. Route 2 at the town offices in Smyrna Mills (founded 1839), easily approached from Interstate 95 from Oakfield, or via Route 2 in Ludlow, about ten miles west of Houlton. From the town offices (set your

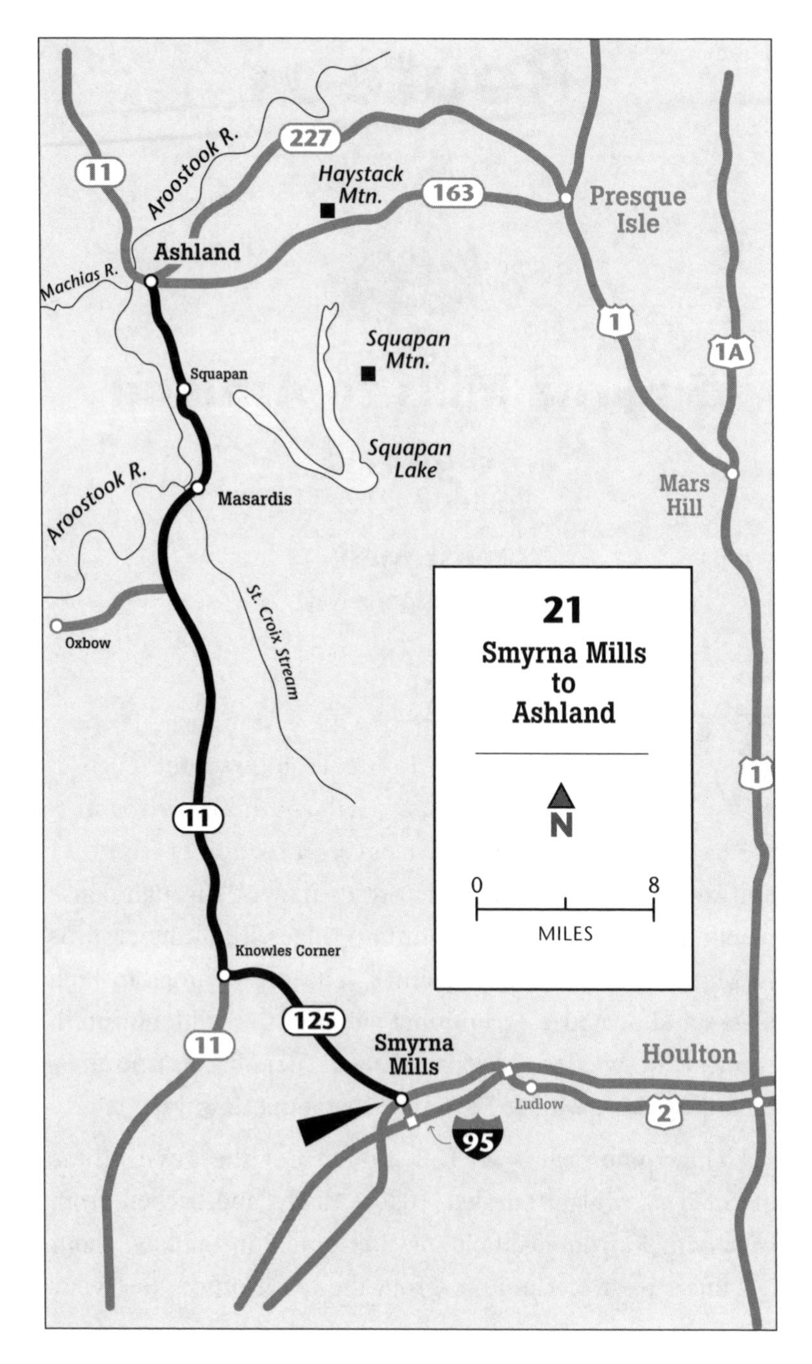
11
Aroostook R.
227
Haystack
Mtn.
163
Presque
Isle
Ashland
Machias R.
1
Squapan
Mtn.
1A
Squapan
Squapan
Lake
Aroostook R.
Masardis
Mars
Hill
Oxbow
St. Croix Stream
21
Smyrna Mills
to
Ashland
N
0
8
MILES
1
11
Knowles Corner
125
11
Smyrna
Mills
Houlton
Ludlow
2
95

odometer here), descend the hill past the United Methodist Church, cross the Bangor & Aroostook railroad tracks, go by the variety store, and come to the junction with Route 125. Go right and northwest here along pretty Cold Brook, immediately entering Merrill at half a mile. Views right toward the brook continue as you head northwest and climb out into high, rolling pasture with splendid views in all directions.

Pass a big dairy farm as you descend northwest and enter woods, then emerge in cultivated acreage and hayfields. The road ascends gradually northwest by more fields and farms with further spectacular views to the west and southwest toward Patten. If you pause and observe, you will see 5,268-foot Mount Katahdin, Maine's highest summit; the Traveler; and other major peaks in Baxter State Park to the southwest. Entering woods again in moose country at 7½ miles, you go by logging roads and run over some roller-coaster terrain, then enter Moro Plantation at 9½ miles. Excellent high outlooks to the north and northeast occur here as you roll to the junction with Route 11 at 10½ miles.

Go right and north now on Route 11 at Knowles Corner, watching for signs indicating Ashland and Eagle Lake. Here you enter T7R5, an unincorporated township, one of many in northwestern Maine. The road passes through bogland dotted with stunted growth and then ascends north through previously cutover ground, and goes by a state rest area on the left at thirteen miles. Some clear-cutting is visible back of the roadside beauty strip. Little marshes lie here and there in this unsettled backcountry, as the road climbs again at 14½ miles. Your route drifts more northwest, visible ahead, as you enter the Frazer Brook flowage and T8R5 at seventeen miles, climbing once more in pretty but heavily cut woodlands.

Yerxa Ridge and Oak Hill lie to the west, and you are only a stone's throw from the Penobscot County line to the west here. At 19¼ miles, you begin a straight descent northward, crossing Boody Brook at 20½ miles, and climb again toward a roadside state rest area. Soon you go by hidden Otter and Matherson Ponds to the left and cross Matherson Brook as you enter T9R5. The road opens up more now in marshy growth, after which you climb again to the northwest. Attractive climax forest lines the way as you level off and run over roller-coaster terrain while approaching another state rest area at 27½ miles. Here you pass a side road to Oxbow and Umcolcus Lodge. The name Oxbow refers to closed stream meanders in the nearby Aroostook River.

Rolling through young spruces, you have mountain views far ahead. Snowmobile trails cross the road, and you enter Masardis at just under thirty miles. Passing Beechnut Sporting Camps, you see more hill views ahead as you next go by the Maine Forest Service station at 31¾ miles and head down into a steep decline in a settlement, crossing St. Croix Stream. Climbing out of town, you are west of unseen Squapan Lake as you pass the road to Squapan Hydro Station, and then drive through some extensive potato fields and, at thirty-four miles, pass a large lumber-milling operation.

Continuing along a high rib, you'll see more excellent views to the left and northwest. You go over the railroad tracks and Squapan Stream at 36½ miles in the tiny settlement of Squapan, then cross the Ashland town line.

Rolling northward through a cutover area, you approach the more settled part of Ashland. More potato fields lie along the right-of-way at thirty-nine miles, and extensive mountain views appear to the west and northwest once more. On clear days, one can see far eastward here, too, with Mars Hill and other low summits visible along the Canadian border. Big barns appear on a high tableland with views across the fields as you descend past bed-and-breakfast places toward town and come into the village (gasoline, shopping, accommodations), reaching a junction with Route 163, the Presque Isle Road, at just under forty-two miles. This drive ends at the top of Ashland's main street at a junction where Route 11 runs left and west toward Portage, and Route 227 leads right toward Frenchville, Castle Hill, and Presque Isle.

To further explore Aroostook, a somewhat longer return south can be made via Route 163 to Presque Isle and U.S. Route 1 to Houlton. While you are here, Ashland is also a good base for further backcountry exploration in the Portage and Eagle Lakes area. Route 11 also continues to the Canadian border at Fort Kent. Gravel paper company roads leave Route 11 farther north for isolated lands to the west. Numerous undeveloped camping places and several comfortable sporting camps lie there in the legendary mountainous region drained by the Allagash and St. John Rivers and interestingly described in such volumes as Helen Hamlin's *Nine Mile Bridge*.

In 1945, backcountry school teacher Hamlin wrote: "To the majority of people, including those who live in the St. John Valley, this forest area is still the mysterious 'backwoods.' A map of the state of Maine shows a large area along the Maine-Canadian boundary that has no highways or towns. It is dotted with lakes and ponds strung along the thin, twisty lines of the St. John and Allagash rivers and their tributaries. There are no highways. There are no towns. . . . The area is approximately 15,600 square miles of woods and lakes, and nothing else." Though road access is far more extensive today and industrial forestry has replaced simpler methods, not much else has changed since Hamlin wrote of her days in timber country.

There are, in fact, more than 26,000 miles of gravel logging roads in Maine, usually approached by gated access points where a small fee is charged for motorized travel in the roughly 2½ million acres of privately owned forest land.

It is also possible to cross westward into Canada on long-distance paper company roads. Ask locally for information or inquire at North Maine Woods. While some paper company roads are very well graded, others are not, requiring travel by vehicles with substantial ground clearance and beefed-up suspensions. If you travel these roads, your car should have a full tank of gas, good tires, adequate ground clearance and be in good repair. There are no auto service facilities in the backcountry.

Route 22

Thompson Island (Bar Harbor)–Pretty Marsh–Bass Harbor–Southwest Harbor–Somesville Loop

Highway:

Route 3, Route 102, Indian Point Road, Route 102A

Distance:

35½ miles (around loop)

Here's a drive that visits the western side of fabled Mount Desert Island, home of Acadia National Park. This corner of Mount Desert is one of the few places on the island anyone should drive in summer, when congestion, particularly around Bar Harbor, can be unpleasant. The west portion of the island tends to be undervisited even in summer, and, in other seasons, seems blissfully lonely. The circuit described here begins and ends at the Thompson Island Information Center on Route 3, just at the entrance to Mount Desert Island. You'll follow a circular route, driving down the extreme west side of the island, across the lower reaches of Mount Desert's western

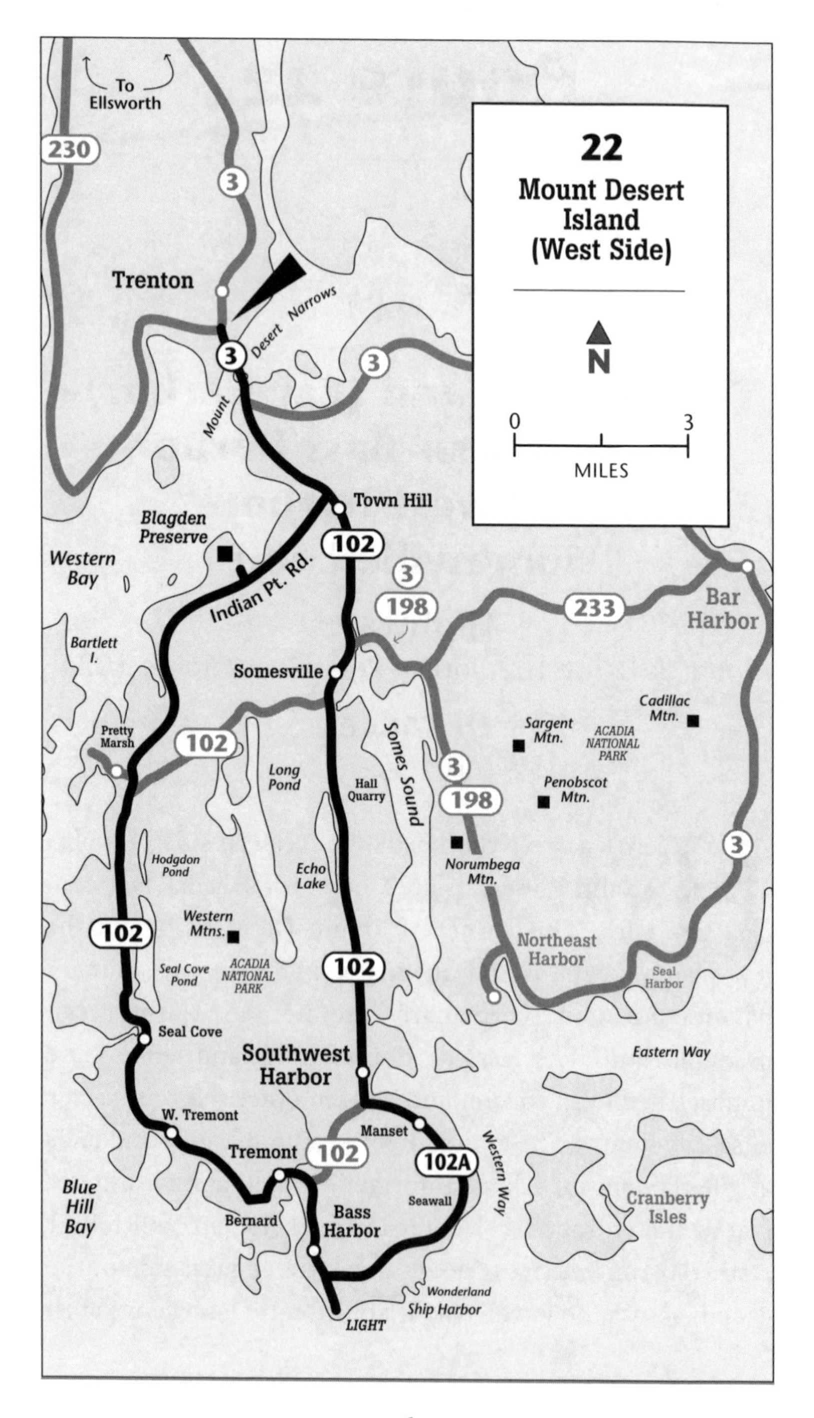
22
Mount Desert Island (West Side)
N
0
3
MILES
To Ellsworth
230
3
Trenton
Mount Desert Narrows
Town Hill
102
Blagden Preserve
Western Bay
Indian Pt. Rd.
198
233
Bar Harbor
Bartlett I.
Somesville
Pretty Marsh
Long Pond
Hall Quarry
Somes Sound
Cadillac Mtn.
Sargent Mtn.
ACADIA NATIONAL PARK
Penobscot Mtn.
Norumbega Mtn.
Hodgdon Pond
Echo Lake
Western Mtns.
Seal Cove Pond
Northeast Harbor
Seal Harbor
Seal Cove
Southwest Harbor
Eastern Way
W. Tremont
Manset
Tremont
102A
Western Way
Blue Hill Bay
Seawall
Bernard
Bass Harbor
Cranberry Isles
Wonderland
Ship Harbor
LIGHT

half, up through Southwest Harbor, and then north along Long Pond and the hills above Somes Sound.

As pretty as this drive is, you must first run the gauntlet of Route 3 from Ellsworth to Trenton and onto Thompson Island. This section of Route 3 has become an ugly honky-tonk, with every conceivable type of hideous tourist trap, but for most people it is the route onto the island. Needless to say, besides the unremitting motels, convenience stores, gift shops, burger stands, and other insults to the eye, traffic here may be reduced to a crawl in summer. If you are approaching from Ellsworth center, an alternative exists. Pick up Route 230 where it crosses U.S. Route 1 (Main Street) in Ellsworth and follow it east and south as it heads for West Trenton and Trenton. Join Route 3 at Trenton, at its junction with Route 230, and you have only a very short drive on Route 3 to Thompson Island Information Center. It is a little longer to Mount Desert from Ellsworth this way, but eminently worth the detour. Route 3 crosses Thompson Island as it goes over Mount Desert Narrows. An information center here has a large parking area, and there are fine views of Oldhouse Cove on Western Bay and of Eastern Bay as you cross the narrows.

From Thompson Island, drive south on Route 3 a few hundred yards and come to a junction with Route 198 and 102. (Set your odometer here.) Keep right on Route 102 at this intersection by Barcadia Campground. Drive south now on Route 102, quickly climbing a hill and pulling away from the junction. The road winds southward in pretty, wooded country. You enter a more built-up area at just over a mile, where you roll through Town Hill village, going through a slump and uphill again. You pass a commercial campground on the left at 1¾ miles. Scaling Town Hill, you turn right on Indian Point Road at two miles. Travel west on Indian Point Road through more wooded country on this winding, narrow way, going by a pasture with horses and through a series of S-curves. The road dips past a boggy pond on the left at 3⅔ miles, heads up another rise, and proceeds farther leftward, going past Oak Hill Road. At just under four miles, you come to the Nature Conservancy's Indian Point–Blagden Preserve on the right. The parking area and headquarters lie just in from the road. Indian Point is a wonderful place to walk northwesterly toward the shore of Western Bay, where, in season, seals may be seen on the rocks. The paths here go through exceptionally pretty woodlands.

Past the Blagden Preserve, the road narrows and winds westerly and southwesterly, climbing gradually and traveling along a plateau at 4¾ miles. Coniferous forest lines the way as you enter another series of bends and head more to the southwest and south, dipping into another hollow. This roller-coaster ride continues for some distance. At 6⅔ miles, you will see a very pretty body of water, known as Goose Marsh Pond, through the trees on the right. Still running southwesterly, go by some pastures and descend to another slump and arrive at a junction with the road from Bartletts Landing at 7¾ miles. Going through a settled area briefly, you pull out into a serpentine and arrive, in a couple of hundred yards, at a junction with Route 102 in Pretty Marsh.

Go right and south at eight miles on Route 102 toward Tremont and Bass Harbor. Drive through a hollow and ascend a rise, entering the town of Tremont at 8¾ miles.

Cross Cape Road in a marsh as the road runs south, with occasional views eastward to the mountains. Fields line the road, and you begin to enjoy water views to the left. The road overlooks two bodies of water, Hodgdon Pond and Seal Cove Pond. Both are striking in appearance, backed by the ledgy mass of Western and Bernard Mountains. As you crest some rolling ribs, there are continuing views to Seal Cove Pond and some marsh views leftward. Places to pull off the road and view this scene lie along here. Fine views toward the boat access point at Seal Cove are seen rightward shortly, at 11½ miles.

You drive by the post office at Seal Cove at 12¾ miles and descend to Murphy Swamp as you head to the left and approach West Tremont. At 13½ miles you pass the West Tremont Methodist Church and then the West Tremont Post Office, working eastward. Occasional good views to the right over Goose Cove and, later, Duck Cove appear. Going through a series of S-curves and climbing a hill, you have southeast water views. At 15¼ miles you pass a commercial campground as the road heads more northeastward, soon arriving at a junction and passing a side road that leads to Bernard. The road goes northeasterly and easterly now, following the upper reaches of Bass Harbor, passing the Tremont Congregational Church with its attractive gingerbread design at 16⅓ miles, with mountain views ahead. Passing more superb water views, you soon arrive at another junction and go right on Route 102A. (Follow signs indicating Swans Island Ferry.)

Route 102A next runs down the east side of Bass Harbor, affording beautiful southward views of the like seen in travelogues. Traditional Maine architecture, bold water exposure, and attractive, wooded countryside make up these quintessential Maine scenes. You enter the little settlement of Bass Harbor, where seasonal accommodations are available. Come to the entrance to Bass Harbor Head Light and keep left at a sharp bend leading to Seawall and Wonderland. (You may wish to first make the drive down to the picturesque lighthouse, the mileage for which is not included in this description. The short side trip is worth the time.)

On Route 102A, at 18½ miles, you pass a commercial campground on the left as you head eastward, and come to the Ship Harbor Nature Trail at nineteen miles. The walk along Ship Harbor offers a very pleasant stroll above the water and takes you out to the open Atlantic through pretty woodlands. Just beyond it, another fine walk in a neighborhood known as Wonderland also invites visitors. Off-road parking is available for both of these walks.

Continuing northeast and north the road goes through a corridor of white spruce encrusted with lichen and, beyond, through an alder swamp, with fine ocean views opening up at 20⅓ miles. You next arrive at a four-way junction by the entrance to Seawall Campground. The picnic area lies to the right; the campground to the left at 20½ miles. Now the road runs along stunningly beautiful, open sea walls along the Atlantic, with Seawall Pond to your left. Seabirds soar over the pond and ocean. You will see the Cranberry Isles offshore to the east.

The route continues northward through the tiny settlement of Seawall and then goes northwest on what is known as Manset Road toward Southwest Harbor. Passing some fields at just under twenty-two miles you will have glimpses northeast toward some of the major peaks on Mount Desert.

Going through Manset at 22¾ miles, you pass the old Gleaners Hall and proceed northwest with more mountain views ahead.

The road heads due west as it nears a junction with Route 102, where you turn right and north on Route 102 (Main Street). In seconds you encounter more spectacular views eastward over Southwest Harbor and to the pink-granite mountains beyond. Full of working and pleasure boats in summer, this busy harbor is a major destination for dedicated East Coast sailors. Passing marinas, rental cottages, inns, motels, stores, and shops, you drive through the center of Southwest Harbor at twenty-four miles.

The last leg of this journey follows Route 102 north with Bernard and Mansell Mountains visible to the west. Pass Seal Cove Road at nearly twenty-five miles and continue toward Thompson Island. This road is usually busier than those you've traveled thus far, but the sights remain attractive. At twenty-five miles, you will find more appealing water views rightward, back toward the ocean. The road climbs a bit now and goes by the trailheads for a number of excellent walks to mountains that overlook beautiful Somes Sound, America's only true fjord.

The Echo Lake entrance to Acadia National Park is on the left at 26½ miles and, just beyond on the right, you'll see the lovely trail to St. Sauveur Mountain. A few yards farther on, the hidden Appalachian Mountain Club Camp lies to the left at nearly twenty-seven miles. There are grand cliffs on

Beech Mountain to the left as you travel by Echo Lake, and arrive at the trailhead for Acadia Mountain at 27⅓ miles.

A rough path in the woods at the trailhead parking lot leads down to a swimming area on Echo Lake. The Ikes Point boat launch area is on the left at 27½ miles, and more fine outlooks down Echo Lake occur at twenty-eight miles.

Passing Pretty Marsh Road at 29¾ miles, you follow Route 102 on to Somesville, a village of very attractive old houses, manicured lawns, and views across Somes Harbor. The Union Meeting House, graceful old stone walls, flower gardens, and a general store lie along Main Street. Leaving this pretty town you pass Babson Creek, with additional fine water views to the mountains eastward, and cross the Bar Harbor town line at 31¾ miles. Drive through open pasture and wooded ground and come to Town Hill village at just under thirty-three miles. Descending northwest, you then pass Indian Point Road, where you started this loop, at 33½ miles, continuing toward Thompson Island. You arrive at the junction of Routes 102 and 3 in a few minutes, at 35½ miles, and bear left on Route 3, going over the causeway to Thompson Island, where this trip ends.

Route 23

West Gouldsboro–Winter Harbor–Schoodic Point–Prospect Harbor–Gouldsboro

Highway:

Route 186, Acadia National Park service road

Distance:

25 miles (around horseshoe)

Yearning for the sea? Well, here is a route that visits the less-frequented and astonishingly lovely section of Acadia National Park that lies east of Frenchman Bay on the Gulf of Maine. The Schoodic Peninsula juts south from the mainland at Gouldsboro, an oceanward plunge of Cadillac granite, jack pines, and spruces. The peninsula delivers outstanding views of the main section of Acadia to the west, the islands to the south, and the open ocean of the Gulf of Maine to eastward. Along the way this route visits several small communities well off the beaten track on lovely coves and harbors. One might say that here is the Maine everyone comes to see, and that most miss.

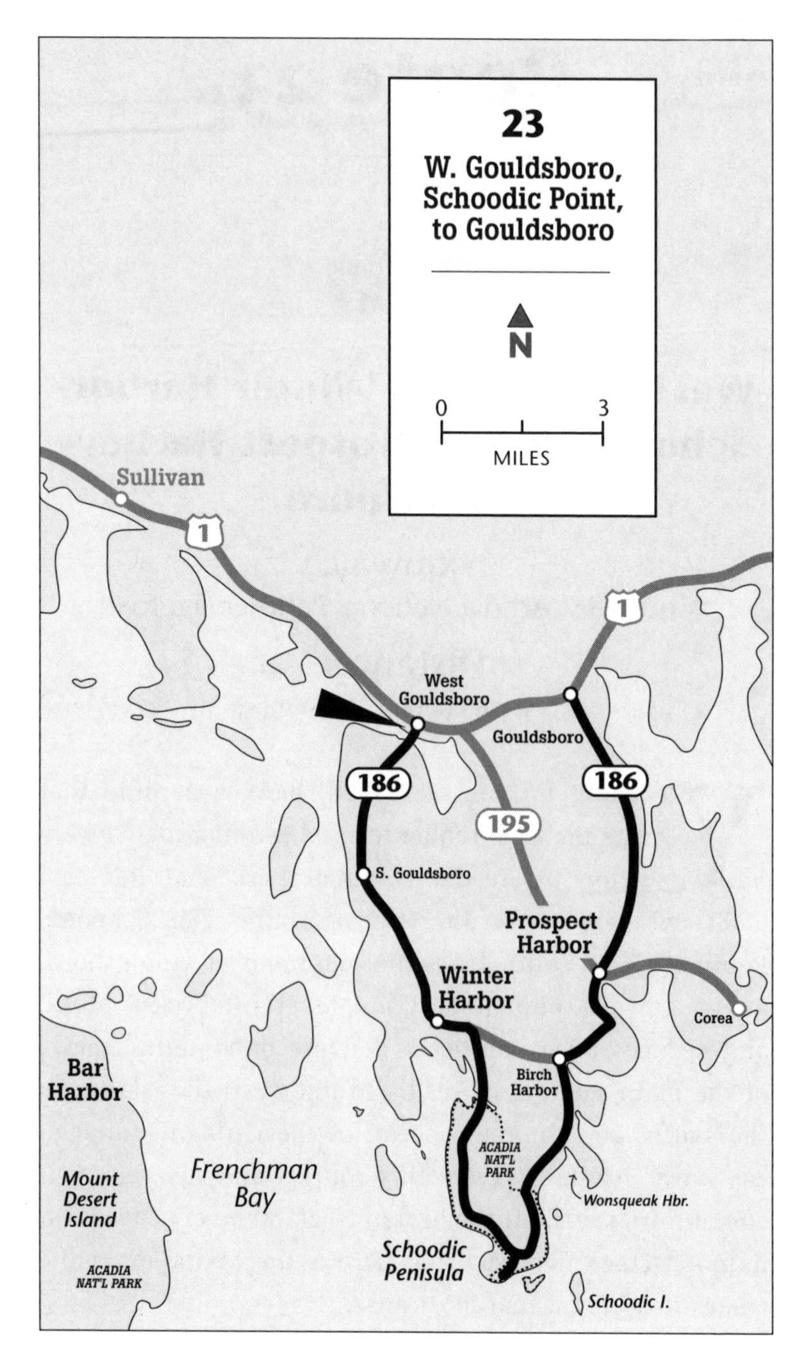

23
W. Gouldsboro, Schoodic Point, to Gouldsboro
N
0
3
MILES
Sullivan
1
1
West Gouldsboro
Gouldsboro
186
186
195
S. Gouldsboro
Prospect Harbor
Winter Harbor
Corea
Birch Harbor
Bar Harbor
ACADIA NAT'L PARK
Mount Desert Island
Frenchman Bay
Wonsqueak Hbr.
Schoodic Penisula
ACADIA NAT'L PARK
Schoodic I.

This journey begins off U.S. Route 1 in West Gouldsboro, 17⅓ miles north of the junction of Route 3 and U.S. Route 1 in Ellsworth. Where U.S. Route 1 and Route 186 meet, go south on Route 186, leaving the traffic behind. Nice old houses and farms give way on the right to excellent vistas over Jones Cove to Hog Island. Stay right on Route 186 at a junction by the Sunset House, go through a settled area by the village library and the West Gouldsboro Union Church, and continue south up a hill. You follow a high rib of land, and go by microwave towers and over some undulating ground, curving sharply left at two miles.

Running more southeasterly, the road heads into rural country, passes a fire station at 2½ miles, and crests a hill with fine views ahead to the Atlantic. Though not yet visible, Frenchman Bay, Bunkers Cove, and Stave Island are to your right as you drive southward here. Go through South Gouldsboro soon and, rising again, take in more hillside views ahead, entering Winter Harbor at just under five miles. There are beautiful water views now as you pass a military housing unit on the left and come to a junction where Route 186 runs left on the verge of the harbor. A local road heads right toward Gerrishville and Grindstone Neck, as you keep left at 6⅓ miles and approach the Schoodic section of Acadia National Park.

Follow signs eastward indicating Birch Harbor on Route 186, leaving the settled area and dropping over a hill to the entrance of the park at a little over seven miles. Bear right here on the park service road, leaving Route 186 for now. Climbing a granite rise dotted with cedars and white spruces, you wind southward, with spectacular rightward

Cadillac granite: the ledges at Schoodic Point

views, enter the park, and pass an entrance to a picnic area on Fraser Point at 8¾ miles. Soon you'll see a lighthouse on Mark Island, and there are broad vistas across the water to Champlain and Cadillac Mountains on Mount Desert Island. Turtle Island and Ledge lie offshore to the west, also. On this one-way highway, there are several convenient turnouts along the shore where you can pull off the road and enjoy the superb views toward Mount Desert and southwest to the Cranberry Isles. Acadia's distinctive, colorful granite is found in abundance in the shoreline ledges and rocks. It fairly glows in the sun.

The road leans away from the water at ten miles and draws southeastward, winding its way to lower ground, and soon again follows the shingle in a lovely cove at eleven miles. Pond Island rests just offshore. Very shortly you arrive at a junction after $11\frac{3}{4}$ miles, where you keep right for a short distance (watch out for two-way traffic here), driving out to the southern tip of the peninsula. You pass the entrance to the U.S. Navy installation and wind westward, coming, at $12\frac{1}{3}$ miles, to a parking area on Big Moose Island, with further perfect views over the Atlantic and Frenchman Bay. The outlooks from these golden granite ledges range over Mount Desert and Bar Harbor, out westward to Egg Rock Light, and southwest toward Frenchboro and Swan's Island. One could hardly exaggerate the magnificence of this scene on a clear day, summer or winter.

Return to the junction, and continue east and right again on the service road at $12\frac{3}{4}$ miles. The route now runs around Arey Cove in one-way traffic, with excellent outlooks toward Little Moose Island and Schoodic Island. Pause at the Blueberry Hill parking area on the right at $13\frac{1}{3}$ miles. A fine hike over Schoodic Head begins opposite the entrance to the parking area. An easy, circular walk of about three miles can be made over the head and back again to this spot. The hike provides spectacular views of Frenchman Bay and Mount Desert and equally good scenes to the east over Wonsqueak and Schoodic Harbors.

From the Blueberry Hill parking area, go right and north again, driving up the east side of the peninsula along Schoodic Harbor. Here are more fine outlooks on the open Atlantic. Superb ledges line the shore, and views extend northeast along the coast toward faraway Jonesport and Great Wass Island. You pass Schoodic Harbor and then Wonsqueak Harbor as you go north.

Maine writer Jonas Crane has argued that the unusual name Wonsqueak has Indian origins. One version of the story claims a beautiful Indian woman was seduced here by a sea serpent in human form of surpassing handsomeness, whom she joined in the sea. The woman still loved her human, land-bound husband, and, missing him, came to shore on moonlit nights, letting out a long, continuous, plaintive screech. The name seems to have later been altered to One Squeak and then to Wonsqueak.

More good cove views emerge at 14¾ miles and, passing a back marsh known as Wonsqueak's Woe, traffic becomes two-way again at 15½ miles as you leave the park. On East Schoodic Drive you pass a commercial campground with more perspectives out over the bays, next reaching a T in quiet Birch Harbor at 17½ miles.

Go right and north here on Route 186 again, and wend your way out of the village to the northeast. The route now drifts eastward and north in a serpentine at 16¾ miles, with more harbor outlooks and a lonely lighthouse at protected Prospect Harbor. You pass the Gouldsboro Fire Station just south of a junction with Route 195, at 19½ miles. Continue north on Route 186 by a store, and pass a side road to Corea, Route 195 eastward, shortly at just under twenty miles.

Mixed-growth forest and brushy fields line the road as you proceed farther north, with water views across fields to Grand Marsh Bay and West Bay. At twenty-four miles, you come to the settled area of Gouldsboro and soon reach the end of this ocean-bound journey at U.S. Route 1 after twenty-five miles of travel.

Route 24

Ellsworth to Cherryfield

Highway:
U.S. Route 1, Route 182

Distance:
23¾ miles (one way)

Most people motoring up or down the Maine coast near Mount Desert Island make their way on U.S. Route 1, U.S. Route 1A, or Route 3. These roads roam close to the coast, and tend to be crowded in summer. At moments they seem to provide more views of tourist traps and motels than of Maine countryside. They also ignore the attractive, quiet country slightly inland and north of Mount Desert Island. Happily, alternatives exist, and they lie in blueberry country.

Back a little from the hurtling bustle of these main routes, travelers can discover the more interesting and unspoiled landscape Dale Rex Coman described in his Pleasant River stories. Of the largely unvisited country north of U.S. Route 1, Coman wrote: "It is a quiet valley, populated more by

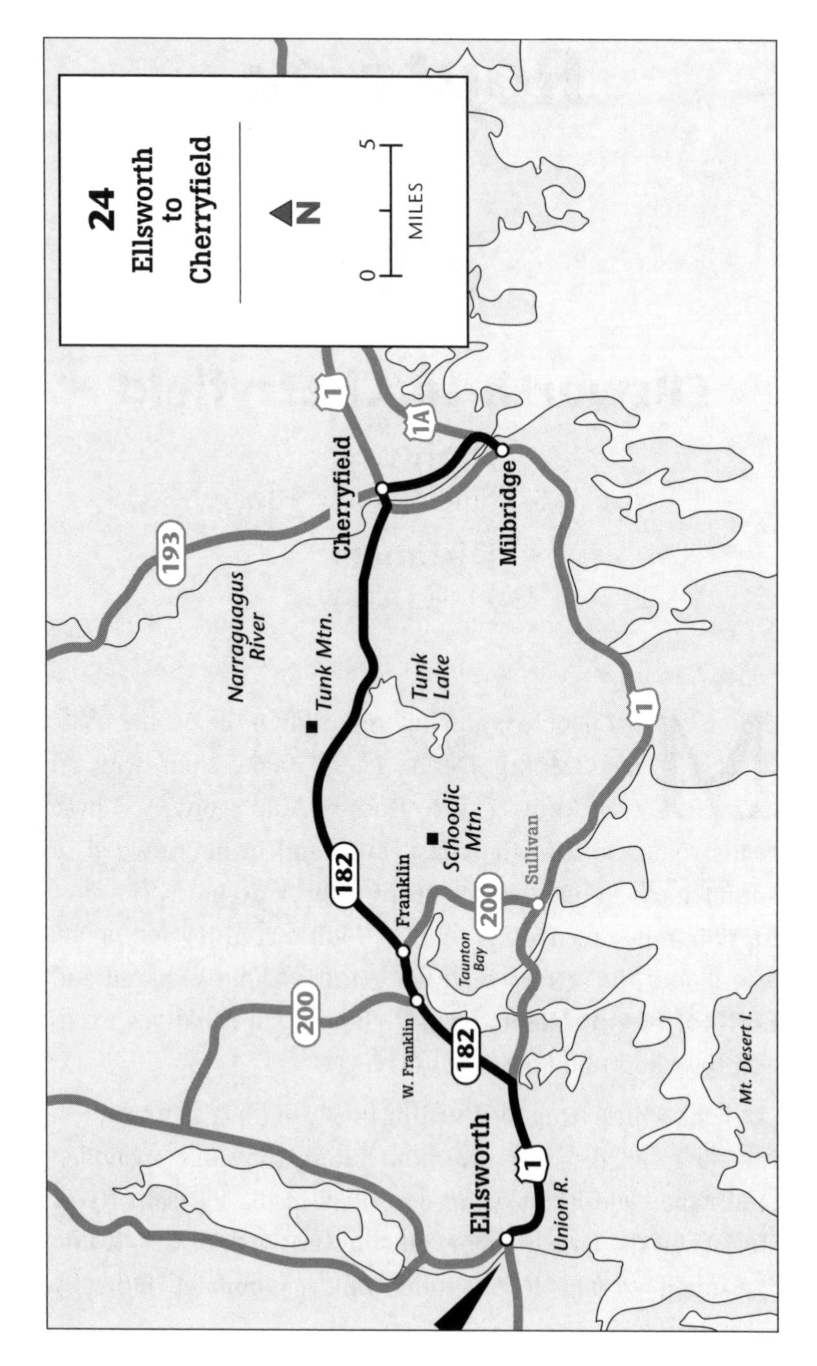
24
Ellsworth
to
Cherryfield
N
0
5
MILES
1
1A
Cherryfield
193
Milbridge
Narraguagus
River
Tunk Mtn.
Tunk
Lake
1
Schoodic
Mtn.
182
Franklin
Sullivan
200
Taunton
Bay
200
W. Franklin
182
Mt. Desert I.
Ellsworth
1
Union R.

deer than people. Here and there one comes upon a deserted homestead, slowly sagging into oblivion as trees and brush creep up on it. The occupants of an occasional farm struggle on, striving to wrest a living from the stony fields and pastures; but they live in an atmosphere that foretells inevitable defeat in the changing ways of our civilization."

This route is one of several whereby one can drive roughly parallel to and either north or south of U.S. Route 1, seeing a lot of fine countryside without the tides of main-road traffic. If you're in a hurry to see how fast you can get from Camden to Calais, this isn't for you. But if you'd like a pleasant ride in this little populated lake country, come along.

Our route begins in Ellsworth, the largest of Maine's five Down East coastal communities of any size. On the Union River, Ellsworth is both an attractive residential community with real downtown shops, restaurants, service agencies, and other necessaries, and also the site of sprawling highway malls and outlets. A walk around Ellsworth's downtown is a nice diversion.

Go east on U.S. Route 1 from Ellsworth's center, coming in a short distance to the junction of U.S. Route 1 and Route 3. Go left and northeast on U.S. Route 1 at this junction. Passing Route 184 shortly, follow U.S. Route 1 several miles through a commercial area, watching carefully for Route 182 on the left about midway between Ellsworth and Hancock. Turn left onto Route 182 (set your odometer now), climb a hill, and head northeast in wooded countryside for West Franklin.

The route goes over a ridge, leaves a settled area, and becomes more rural as you cross the Franklin town line at 2⅔ miles. There are striking views of tidal Egypt Bay to the right here, with views ahead of rolling fields and the tip of nearby Schoodic Mountain. More fine water views of Taunton Bay occur on the right at 3¾ miles, backed by the profile of Schoodic Mountain once again. Going through some marshland, you arrive after five miles at a junction with Route 200 in West Franklin. Continue northeast on Route 182, passing the Franklin Community Center at 5¾ miles, with still more water views rightward over Hog Bay.

Going next through Franklin village, a tiny community of attractive older homes, stay left by the Franklin Baptist Church on Route 182 where Route 200 goes right. Occasional glimpses of Schoodic Mountain and, above it, Black and Caribou Mountains, appear to eastward. You go by the Franklin Trading Post (gasoline) and post office at just under seven miles. The road winds northeastward in sparsely settled woods, climbing hills and descending into ridges with good outlooks on both sides of the pavement at 8½ miles.

Passing over Martin Ridge Brook and then more rolling hills, you find mountain views appear again in spruce and pine woodlands as you enter Township 9 at 10⅓ miles. Heading more eastward now, you travel through rocky woods grown up in oak in Township 10 at twelve miles. This is wild, unsettled country, devoid of houses, and the winding road demands close attention to one's driving. Luckily, little traffic occurs here. Take in the broad views of Gill Bog on the right shortly, and at 13¼ miles arrive at the head of beautiful Fox Pond. The road follows the shore here, with splendid outlooks across the water for some distance.

Tunk Lake and surrounding hills

Cresting a height of land at 15⅓ miles, you'll have excellent lake and mountain views ahead on a steep grade.

You descend now to a rest area on Tunk Lake on the right at 16⅔ miles. Expansive lake and mountain scenery lies to the south of this shaded cedar grove. Blackwood, Peaked, Black, and Catherine Mountains rise behind the lake. A stream here connects with Spring River Lake to the north, and small boats can be launched on Tunk Lake from this cove. This spot makes a supremely pleasant place to pause, relax, and perhaps have lunch on a sunny day in the warmer months.

Your route now winds east again, running through a marshy area, leaving spruce, hemlock, and juniper forest for stands of oaks and maples. Attractive Long Pond appears to the south in moments at 18¾ miles. Cross the Washington County line into Cherryfield at just under twenty miles. You'll see the ledgy ridge known as Burke Hill, and the road widens out in a built-up area as you come into the village.

Settled in 1757, Cherryfield bills itself as the "blueberry capital of the world," and no community elsewhere seems at all disposed to challenge that legend. Though they exist over a wide area in eastern Maine, this is the heart of Maine's commercial blueberry fields.

Pass a side road to Unionville at 22½ miles and descend to the junction with U.S. Route 1. Turn left and north here and, in just a few hundred yards, you are in Cherryfield center, a cluster of appealing old buildings by the bridge that spans the Narraguagus River. The Narraguagus flows a considerable distance down from Jimmies Pond, the Allen Ponds, Bracey Pond, Lovejoy Pond, and the extensive marshes below Nicatous Lake. Here at the bridge, it runs to the sea barely five miles southward at Milbridge. This trip ends here at the junction of U.S. Route 1 and Route 193.

For those interested in a rewarding little side trip, take the Kansas Road, which is a continuation of Route 193, south from U.S. Route 1 at Cherryfield center. Follow this road southward on high bluffs over the east side of the Narraguagus to Milbridge and Narraguagus Bay. Milbridge was one of those tiny northern settlements that played a role in the constant attempts of British, French, and even Dutch authorities to control this stretch of valuable coastal terrain before and after the Revolution. Local resistance was by turns stirred up by each of these great powers, depending on the state of political affairs in Europe and interest in colonial exploitation.

From 1764, Major Joseph Wallace was the preeminent Revolutionary-period shipbuilder here amongst a gathering of shipbuilding families, including Leightons, Sawyers,

Gays, Dyers, and Hinckleys. French ships attacked a harbor full of Wallace-built ships at anchor in 1807, and destroyed this small fleet and the Wallace shipyards. The family soon rebuilt, and Wallace ships were a factor against the British in the War of 1812.

As locals were forbidden to take fish from these north-coast waters, certain feisty individuals got their backs up. One of the most legendary of these was "Gunpowder" Beal from the island of that name. A coastal settler of enormous proportions and strength, Beal fished Washington County coastal shoals during the War of 1812, and was harassed by British customs officers and the troops that supported them. When approached by a boatload of armed British troops, Gunpowder Beal threw a fishing net over their long-boat and, using his immense strength, grabbed the gunwales of their craft and violently rocked it back and forth until the British were nearly swamped, discouraged, and not a little seasick. Beal had justified his nickname as a man of potentially explosive temper, and the British, duly warned, henceforth left him alone.

Add five miles to your total travel distance if you make this side trip to Milbridge.

Route 25

East Machias–Cutler–Lubec–West Quoddy Head

Highway:

Route 191, Route 189, South Lubec Road

Distance:

36½ miles (one way)

Machias and East Machias perch on the farther limits of Maine's coast, where several rivers, creeks, and brooks enter Machias Bay on the northern fringe of the Gulf of Maine. This is well-weathered, no-nonsense country, tangy with the flavor of Down East, rough terrain, isolation, and a hardscrabble existence. Fishing, wreath-making, growing blueberries, logging, and not much else form the underpinnings of the region's economy. And though eastern Washington County is more prosperous than it once was, certainly more so than when my grandfather and grandmother lived out their lives up the road in Calais, it's still pretty basic country. You live here because you like it the way it is; anywhere else would seem silly, frivolous.

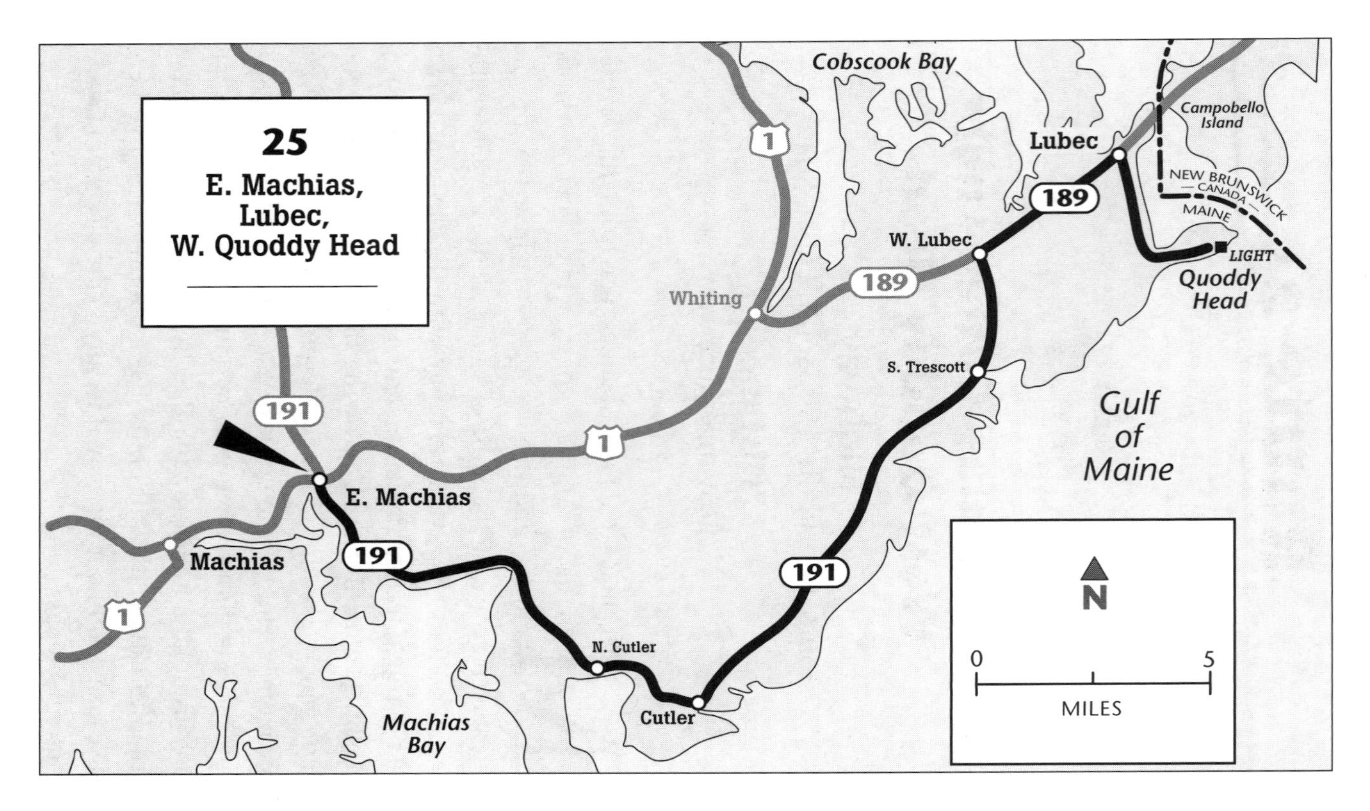
25
E. Machias,
Lubec,
W. Quoddy Head
Campobello Island
NEW BRUNSWICK
— CANADA —
MAINE
LIGHT
Quoddy Head
Lubec
189
Gulf of Maine
Cobscook Bay
W. Lubec
S. Trescott
189
191
1
Whiting
Cutler
N. Cutler
1
E. Machias
191
Machias Bay
191
Machias
1
N
0
5
MILES

Where Washington County meets the sea it finds its saving grace in a kind of natural, sere beauty—summer and winter—that exists nowhere else. It is a beauty you have to adjust the eye to recognize, not the lush, slick attractiveness conjured up in the pages of travel magazines. And then, at the end of this journey, lies that great coil of land and water where the Dennys, Pennamaquan, and Orange Rivers empty into Dennys, Cobscook, and Whiting Bays. At Lubec, the neck of land known as West Quoddy Head juts into the cold Atlantic, a long stone's throw from Canada. Here, east of east, Quoddy's lighthouse guards the Grand Manan Channel.

To experience this appealing corner of Down East Maine, begin in East Machias where Route 191 crosses U.S. Route 1 at an old dam and heads south. Follow Route 191 south past the attractive First Congregational Church, go through a residential neighborhood and by Washington Academy (1823). There are views of the East Machias River to the right from Route 191 as you descend southeast in a section known as Dog Town.

Backmarshes appear at one mile, and sheep and cows graze on nearby hillsides as you cross Cripple Creek at $1\frac{1}{3}$ miles. There are additional satisfying views back to the west and leftward over marshland at $2\frac{1}{2}$ miles. Farther on, these superb ocean views broaden to the southwest and south over Little Bay and Holmes Bay as you round Enoch Hill.

One of the earliest direct actions of the Revolutionary War occurred in these waters. In June 1775, a group of Machias rebels led by Jeremiah O'Brien, Benjamin Foster, and George Stillman stormed and took the British four-gunner *Margaretta*, which had sailed up the coast as escort to the *Unity* and *Polity*. These two sloops, owned by Machiasman Ichabod Jones, were full of supplies for the hard-pressed Machias community, and were allowed to land only on condition that they be immediately loaded with timber and sent back to the British in Boston. The rebels could not countenance this blackmail, and thus raided the gunner. The British midshipman in command lost his life to a rebel fowling gun, and new America had its first naval victory.

Cross the Whiting town line at nearly five miles as the grand, sweeping bay views continue, and head eastward through a more settled area. At 6½ miles, you run more to the south, cross Holmes Stream, and go over the Cutler town line at 6¾ miles. You cross Huntley Creek shortly. The road now descends due southeast in pretty countryside to North Cutler, where you will see a U.S. Navy Communications installation, with its waterside forest of giant rhombic antennas that thrust out toward Thornton Point. A corridor of mixed-growth woodlands borders Route 191 as you run up and down a series of ribs, soon coming to some interesting bogs with standing dead trees and swamps dense with alder, followed by further spectacular views over Little Machias Bay to the south at ten miles.

Crossing an inlet over Eastern Marsh Spring Brook, climb a hill into Cutler at 11½ miles, going by the Head of the River Baptist Church. Come down Cutler's Main Street with excellent views toward the open ocean over the Little River and Eastern Nubble. Fishing boats dot the superb harbor, and small, snug houses line the high hillside above the water. You'll pass the town offices and library at

Eastward over Cutler Harbor

12¾ miles, followed by docks where Route 191 goes sharply left and northeast. Going uphill by the fire station, you travel northward on 191 toward Trescott. You are quickly back in dense spruce woods and on to an alder swamp as you drive out of town in the kind of wild, rough country so typical of Washington County.

Low-bush blueberry fields lie to the left, and you cross over Schooner Brook and drive by French Ridge. The stream stays to the right as you go through barren, marshy fields where muskrat lodges hide in the dense grass. At 17½ miles, you reach the parking area for the Cutler Coastal Preserve, an unspoiled, thickly wooded preserve with outstanding walking trails down to and along the high bluffs over Black Point and Long Point Coves. The cliffs in this preserve are arguably the most outstanding on the Atlantic coast accessible to walkers. These coastal cliffs, bordered by eighteen-foot tides, are backed by high heathlands and dense spruce woods. A delightful and challenging five-mile circuit of the headlands can be made from this point.

Beyond the Cutler Coastal Trail, you continue north toward South Trescott in ever wilder countryside, in woods thick with spruces, aspens, hackmatacks, and little else. Blueberry fields appear from time to time as the road meanders up and down northward and you pass beautiful, isolated marshes with not a house in sight. At twenty miles, enter Trescott on winding pavement and, passing abandoned farmhouses, soon descend to Moose Cove, an ocean inlet that forms a lovely rounded body of water to the right at 23¾ miles. Crest another hill, and you'll see the road you're traveling ahead. Hills loom in the distance. In minutes, you drive by Haycock Harbor, go through minuscule South Trescott, and run past the harbor known as Bailey's Mistake (Bailey was bound for some-where else). You reach the junction with Route 189 at 27½ miles, in West Lubec.

Going right and northeast toward Lubec through a built-up area on Route 189, pass the West Lubec United Methodist Church on the left at just under twenty-eight miles. Limited accommodations and food service are available on this road. Pass the Ridge Baptist Church in a more settled area at thirty-one miles, with occasional views to the southeast toward the ocean. Better outlooks soon appear toward the Atlantic across Lubec Channel. Other water views appear to the left over South Bay and then Johnson Bay. At 31¾ miles, bear right on South Lubec Road, watching for signs indicating West Quoddy Head.

Go south on this road through a residential area, passing the buildings of the Regional Medical Center at Lubec. There are fine water views eastward toward West Quoddy Head and Grand Manan, and marsh views to the right as

East of east: West Quoddy Head Light backed by Grand Manan

you drive along. Back to the left, connected to Lubec by a modern, high bridge, is Campobello Island, once the summer residence of President Franklin Delano Roosevelt. The road heads southeast and goes by several more houses, and then bears sharply northeastward and left toward West Quoddy Head at 34½ miles. You drive through a raised heath with excellent views up the channel toward Lubec proper. The bridge to Campobello is clearly visible. The road soon climbs eastward and winds through dense spruce forest, arriving shortly at the parking area by West Quoddy Head Light at 36½ miles.

West Quoddy Head Light, the easternmost in America, is now maintained by the State of Maine. The U.S. Coast Guard has divested itself of its lighthouses with fire-sale rapidity. Private groups, state agencies, and preservationists have been active in attempting to keep the lights alive now that the cash-starved Coast Guard has departed. The red stripes on the Quoddy's handsome profile are identifying markings for navigators. From the grounds around the lighthouse and nearby trails one looks out on spectacular vistas that include the Grand Manan Channel, Campobello Island, and the long, low island profile of Grand Manan, where the author's grandmother was born and raised. Ledges radiate outward from the height on which the lighthouse rests. Everywhere there is water: the cold, eccentric currents of surrounding bays, the channel, and the open Atlantic.

Adjacent Quoddy Head State Park offers a network of excellent hiking paths that follow the contours of this dramatic and distinctive headland. Picnic areas and toilet facilities are available.

Persons using the trails, especially families with small children, should use care on those trail sections that closely follow the precipices that line the east side of the Head. Unprotected trails are, in some places, very close to the edge of high terrain over the sea cliffs. Caution should be observed.